C000127974

YORK NOTES

General Editors: Professor A.N. J.......
of Stirling) & Professor Suheil Bushrui (*American
University of Beirut*)

William Shakespeare

CORIOLANUS

Notes by Andrew Gurr

MA (AUCKLAND) PH D (CAMBRIDGE)
Professor of English, University of Reading

**LONGMAN
YORK PRESS**

YORK PRESS
Immeuble Esseily, Place Riad Solh, Beirut.

LONGMAN GROUP UK LIMITED
Longman House, Burnt Mill, Harlow,
Essex CM20 2JE, England
Associated companies, branches and representatives
throughout the world

First published 1980
Seventh impression 1993

ISBN 0-582-03343-8

Produced by Longman Singapore Publishers Pte Ltd
Printed in Singapore

Contents

Part 1: Introduction   *page*   5

  Shakespeare's life   5

  Shakespeare's theatre   10

  Roman history and politics   14

  A note on the text   17

Part 2: Summaries   18

  A general summary   18

  Detailed summaries   21

Part 3: Commentary   56

  Political questions   56

  Structure   58

  Language   59

  Tragedy   60

  Stage history   61

Part 4: Hints for study   62

  An outline of a study plan   62

  Specimen questions and answers   63

Part 5: Suggestions for further reading   68

The author of these notes   71

Part 1

Introduction

Shakespeare's life

William Shakespeare, the greatest writer in English, was born in April 1564 at Stratford-upon-Avon. Stratford, in the fertile farming country of Warwickshire near the geographical centre of England, is about ninety miles from London and in the sixteenth century was a small market town. Shakespeare's father was a prominent citizen, a magistrate, and at one time mayor, whose living came by making gloves, buying and selling wool and in other kinds of small business dealing. Shakespeare's mother came from a family of landowners rather more wealthy than the family into which she married. Neither side of Shakespeare's parentage had any pretension to high social status, though his father did acquire a coat of arms in 1596, which authorised him to call himself a 'gentleman'.

William, the eldest son of a family of six, was probably educated at the local grammar school in Stratford. He married in November 1582 when he was only eighteen. His wife was a 25-year-old girl from a neighbouring village. They had three children, a daughter in 1583 and a twin boy and girl in 1585. Apart from these bare facts no records of Shakespeare exist until after he had begun to make a name in London in 1592 as an aspiring playwright. His father's business started to do badly when William was in his teens. He may have been for that reason driven to seek his fortune in London, or he might equally well have wanted to see what the world beyond Stratford and his family was like. Whichever his motive was, he found himself a form of employment— play-acting—which kept him in London and away from his family for more than twenty years. Not until 1609, when he was forty-five, did he return to his wife and children to live in peaceful retirement with them until his death in 1616.

He retired to Stratford a wealthy man. He made a good deal of money from his acting and playwriting, and took care to invest almost all of it in Stratford. By 1597 he had bought the second largest house in town for his wife to live in, and by the time he retired to it he also owned several hundred acres of farmlands adjoining the town

Shakespeare's career in London, where nearly all his thirty-seven plays were written, was highly prosperous from 1594 onwards. Before that he struggled for some years to make his way. His main occupation was acting (the first definite reference to him, in 1592, calls him contemptuously 'in his own conceit the only Shake-scene in a country'). Working with one of the travelling companies or if he was lucky with a company based in London, Shakespeare's daily occupation, from which he made his regular income, was as an actor. He wrote his plays in his spare time and made money from them by hiring them out for performance by his acting company. Unlike most of his contemporaries he did not sell the plays he wrote to the actors. If he had not kept them he could not have handed over in 1594 the eight or nine plays he had by then written to his new company, the Chamberlain's Men.

The financial climate for actors was harsh before 1594. Epidemics of plague kept forcing the London theatres to close, and acting companies 'broke and went into the country', as it was described, with depressing regularity. Shakespeare seems not to have liked travelling as a player and to have clung to London. In 1593 and early 1594 he made a bid for fame as a poet, publishing the poems *Venus and Adonis* and *The Rape of Lucrece* as his show-pieces. Meanwhile his plays were hired out to various acting companies. *Titus Andronicus* (1590?) records on the title page of its 1594 edition that it was performed by three different companies. Poetry, however, proved insufficient as a livelihood, and in mid-1594 Shakespeare joined a newly formed company and stayed with it as it rose to pre-eminence. This company, the Chamberlain's Men, was made up of some of the best actors of the day. Its leading man, Richard Burbage, was not only a rising star but he was also a son of the owner of the first playhouse built in London. His new company therefore in 1594 had an automatic monopoly of one of the three playing venues.

Shakespeare became a shareholder in the new acting company. He bought his share either with cash given him by the Earl of Southampton, the patron to whom he dedicated his poems, or with the plays he had already written. These included the first tetralogy of plays which he based on English history, the three *Henry VI* plays and *Richard III* (1593), *Titus Andronicus*, and several comedies, including *The Comedy of Errors* (1590?), *The Taming of the Shrew* (1591?), and *Two Gentlemen of Verona* (1592?). The years after 1594 were very prosperous ones for the London-based companies. They were able to perform continuously, almost without interruption from the plague, for nearly eight years. Shakespeare's wealth grew greatly in this time. Soon he became not only a shareholder in the company but a householder, a part-owner of the new playhouse, the Globe, built on the south bank of the Thames as a permanent home for the company in 1597.

In these early years of the Chamberlain's Men's first prosperity, when they were the foremost of the foremost, the best of the three companies allowed to perform regularly in London, Shakespeare's work went from strength to strength. His plays were regularly performed at Court, and some, notably the Falstaff plays and *Hamlet*, became the most popular of the time. Apart from his acting, which probably did not involve him in leading roles, he seems to have provided his company with two plays a year, one serious and one comic, every year for fifteen years. His serious plays at first extended the run of plays based on English history, with the sequence which runs from *Richard II* (1595) through the two *Henry IV* plays (1596–7) to *Henry V* (1599). Then he began a series on Roman history with *Julius Caesar* (1599) but broke it off to write the great tragedies, beginning with *Hamlet* in 1600. His comedies included *A Midsummer Night's Dream* (1595?), *The Merchant of Venice* (1596), and that scintillating group, the most purely comic he wrote, *Much Ado about Nothing, As You Like It* and *Twelfth Night, or What You Will* (1598–1600).

When James I came to the throne in 1603 he acknowledged the status of the leading companies by allowing his family to become their patrons. Shakespeare's company became the King's Men, its nearest rival became the Queen's Men and the third company became the Prince's Men. From this time on, until the Parliamentary party shut down all theatres in 1642 at the beginning of the English Revolution, the King's Company was the outstanding acting troupe, possessing (in Shakespeare's thirty-seven plays) the outstanding repertoire of all time. *Othello, King Lear, Macbeth*, the so-called problem comedies and the last Roman plays, *Antony and Cleopatra* and *Coriolanus*, were added to their lists in this period. In 1608 they gained a new resource, another theatre, the Blackfriars, which Shakespeare invested in as he had in their main theatre, the Globe. The Blackfriars had in fact originally been constructed by the Burbages in 1596, when the company hoped to have both a large open-air amphitheatre (the Globe) and an enclosed hall inside the city walls for winter performances (the Blackfriars). Local opposition stopped them from using the Blackfriars hall at first, and it was first used as a theatre by a company of boy actors. When they failed Shakespeare's company repossessed it for their own use. Thereafter they acted in it for eight months of the year and at the outdoor Globe through the summer months.

Shakespeare, although he kept rooms in the Blackfriars gatehouse only 200 yards from the new theatre, withdrew from his day-to-day commitments as actor and playwright soon after the Blackfriars came back to the company. He retired to Stratford, and thereafter wrote only a few more plays (*The Winter's Tale, The Tempest,* and *Henry VIII,* of which he seems to have written little more than half), and probably lent a hand in writing others. He died, wealthy and famous, at his home in Stratford, more or less on the anniversary of his birth, in April 1616. As the most substantial of his memorials his fellow actors gathered up almost all of his plays, thirty-six of them, and published them in one huge volume in 1623, the edition known as the First Folio.

Like the other great dramatists of his time, Christopher Marlowe, Ben Jonson and Thomas Middleton, Shakespeare came from a social level which, a century earlier, would never have had access to the education which was the prerequisite for their writing. Nor, before the growth of a market for printed books and an audience for plays in commercial theatres, could they have made a living from their talents. Shakespeare might well have stayed in Stratford all his life helping with his father's business enterprises. As it was, he prospered by his pen more than any of his contemporaries. Nonetheless the early years must have been painful and precarious. He must have been very familiar with the mood described in Sonnet 29:

> *When in disgrace with Fortune and men's eyes,*
> *I all alone beweep my outcast state,*
> *And trouble deaf heaven with my bootless cries,*
> *and look upon myself, and curse my fate,*
> *Wishing me like to one more rich in hope,*
> *Featur'd like him, like him with friends possess'd,*
> *Desiring this man's art, and that man's scope,*
> *With what I most enjoy contented least . . .*

His attempt to establish himself through poetry as an alternative to the uncertainties of an acting career indicates how uncomfortable he found his life to be in those years. The sonnet however is not truly an expression of misery. It gives a coolly precise description of a bleak mood out of which, he goes on to say, he can easily lift himself:

> *Yet in these thoughts myself almost despising,*
> *Haply I think on thee, and then my state,*
> *Like to the lark at break of day arising*
> *From sullen earth, sings hymns at heaven's gate.*

For every pressure in one direction, there is a balancing counter-pressure. Balance, and the control exercised by a mind capable of acknowledging every pressure without failing under it, are the supreme qualities of Shakespeare's mind.

Considering how much he wrote, we have strikingly little in the way of clues to Shakespeare's thought. His plays are almost totally devoid of personal references, and even the few details which do seem to arise out of his own life—for instance the riot over the shortage of corn which opens *Coriolanus* and which can be related to riots in his own Warwickshire over the price of food in 1607—give little hint of what he thought about them. So balanced is his presentation of themes and characters in his plays that critics have found it possible to argue with equal justice, or rather with equal injustice, in favour of quite opposed points of view. It has been argued, for instance, that in *Julius Caesar* Shakespeare approves of Caesar, and on the other hand with equal force that he shows disapproval of him. The current consensus is that he carefully balances the medieval view which condemned Caesar and the Renaissance view which approved of him. Similarly, the stage history of *Coriolanus* shows that audiences and critics have found in it either sympathy for the patricians, and consequently a condemnation of the citizens, or the reverse. It is in the nature of drama that it conceals the author's own opinion behind the opinions of his characters.

The only evidence about Shakespeare's mind, the only really direct expression of his views, survives in his sonnets. A collection of 154 of them was published in 1609, most likely without his permission. The majority were written long before that, probably in the 1590s while he was establishing his reputation as poet and playwright in London. Most of them, 126 in all, are addressed to a young man, and form a sequence of letters in verse. We do not know the identity of the young man, though some of his features are apparent from references made in individual sonnets. He was young, handsome, wealthy and of a very high social standing. The first sonnets were commissioned by the young man's mother, and urge him to marry and produce children. Soon, however, they become much more direct love poems, as the relationship between the poet and his subject deepens. The poet laments the fact that he is so much older, and in such an inferior social position that their friendship has to be kept secret. Sonnet 29, quoted above, says the young man is the joy in his life. For his part the young man is cooler. He casually insults the poet and gets in reply a cutting reproof (Sonnet 33), which leads to a cautious reconciliation. In Sonnets 40–2 however the poet is shattered by a double betrayal: his own mistress seduces the young man. That offence too is healed, and the relationship becomes a loving one in a more complex, careful way. Later the young man shows a preference for a rival poet, and later still, near the end of the sequence, the poet himself seems to have committed a betrayal similar to the first offence of the young man. The relationship evidently lasted over several years, and seems in some respects to have been at the core of Shakespeare's emotional life. The relations between poet and young aristocrat seem to be curiously like those of Falstaff to Prince Hal in the *Henry IV* plays.

Shakespeare's relations with his mistress followed a quite different pattern. Most of the remainder of the sonnets are to or about her. She is described as 'black' in contrast to the 'fair' which meant beautiful. One particularly cutting sonnet (131) says that she is not really ugly—'In nothing art thou black, save in thy deeds, And thence this slander, as I think, proceeds.' Two of the sonnets are addressed to her about her seduction of the young man, and another describes the two of them as his good and evil angels, 'a man right fair', and 'a woman colour'd ill'. She is promiscuous—'the wide world's common place'—and is another man's wife. The sonnets express the torments of a simultaneous lust for her body and loathing of her actions.

These hints about the playwright's private life are tantalising because they offer such brief glimpses of the experience he drew on for his plays. Superb as the plays are, in their understanding of human nature and their command of all the varieties of language, they have been used as evidence of a bewildering variety to explain his incredible mind. The imagery he uses shows familiarity with so many walks of life that it has been conjectured he must have worked as a farmer, a teacher, a lawyer, a soldier, a seaman and many other occupations besides the one we know he had, an actor. He knew, as his friend and fellow playwright Ben Jonson rather patronisingly put it, 'small Latin and less Greek', but he could if need be read texts in Latin, French and Italian, and had an encyclopaedic knowledge of English history and philosophy. Few writers show greater understanding of—as distinct from mere knowledge of—the currents of thought in his time. He has been described by a historian as the greatest of Tudor historians, and a recent book (Paul A. Cantor, *Shakespeare's Rome*, Cornell University Press, Ithaca, 1976) maintains that in his Roman plays his knowledge of Roman government and society, even with the limited sources available to him, shows a profound understanding from which we, for all our superior knowledge of detail, have still a great deal to learn.

Shakespeare's theatre

The acting world in which Shakespeare worked and the milieu of the theatre for which his plays were composed are crucial to an understanding of his work. In Sonnet 111 he writes that his nature is almost 'subdued/To what it works in, like the dyer's hand'. Not only are the plays packed with images from the theatre, 'playing', and 'acting', but the idea that all the world's a stage clearly shaped much of his thinking. The relationship between reality and illusion is acknowledged at every level in his writing. Furthermore, apart from the two long poems he published in 1593 and 1594, the only form in which he chose to display his art was the stage. Less than a third of his plays appeared in print in his lifetime, and none of those that did were printed with his approval. If it had not been for the devotion of his fellow actors in printing the First Folio in 1623 many of his plays, including *Macbeth, Antony and Cleopatra, Coriolanus* and *The Tempest*, would never have survived. His plays were written for performance, not for reading.

This is extraordinary, if only because the performances even of Shakespeare's own company were by our standards rushed and unsubtle. The company consisted of ten, and later twelve, chief actors, the shareholders. Casting the parts was fairly automatic—one actor would play old men's parts, another a soldier's, a third was the clown, Burbage was the hero, and so on. Each leading actor had an apprentice in his care, and the apprentices would take the female roles. Hired men played the walk-on parts, a typical performance involving between twenty and twenty-four men altogether, with some doubling of the minor speaking parts. Directing was rudimentary. A prompter or 'book-keeper' sat behind the stage to remind actors of their cues and to make sure the necessary properties were on hand. There was no fixed scenery, and little spectacle that was not portable, in the form of either costumes or of properties such as thrones, tables, and benches which could be carried on stage as they were needed. Shakespeare seems hardly ever to have intervened to make sure that his plays were staged and his words spoken as he had intended when he wrote them. The normal time for a performance was two hours, which meant that both words and action must have galloped along. Modern performances take at least three hours.

In a busy repertory company there was in any case little room for refinements. A successful company would expect to perform every afternoon of the week except Sundays, and every week of the year, plague permitting, except for the six weeks of Lent, the Christian fast before Easter which included abstinence from such pleasures as play-going. Usually the play would be a different one each day, so that the players would be constantly learning their parts for new plays or brushing up their old ones. The stage at the open-air Globe projected out into the 'yard', the centre of the amphitheatre, where the audience who paid the smallest amount of entrance money stood. Spectators who were kept standing all through the two hours of a performance, and who clustered around the five-foot-high stage platform itself as closely

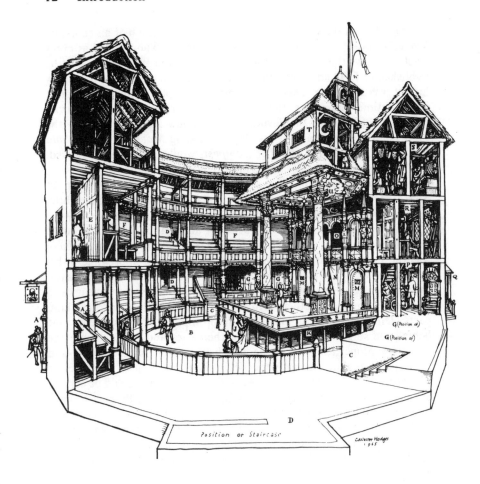

A CONJECTURAL RECONSTRUCTION OF THE INTERIOR OF THE GLOBE PLAYHOUSE

AA Main entrance
 B The Yard
CC Entrances to lowest gallery
 D Entrance to staircase and upper galleries
 E Corridor serving the different sections of the middle gallery
 F Middle gallery ('Twopenny Rooms')
 G 'Gentlemen's Rooms' or Lords' Rooms'
 H The stage
 J The hanging being put up round the stage
 K The 'Hell' under the stage
 L The stage trap, leading down to the Hell
MM Stage doors

 N Curtained 'place behind the stage'
 O Gallery above the stage, used as required sometimes by musicians, sometimes by spectators, and often as part of the play
 P Back-stage area (the tiring-house)
 Q Tiring-house door
 R Dressing-rooms
 S Wardrobe and storage
 T The hut housing the machine for lowering enthroned gods, etc., to the stage
 U The 'Heavens'
 W Hoisting the playhouse flag

as they could, would need to be kept entertained by a constant barrage of speech and action. So the performances were fast and noisy, with little time to dwell on sentimental or dramatic moments. Beer, fruit and nuts were on sale during the performance, too—there was no interval—so the actors' voices had to compete against a background of shuffling feet, cracking nuts, and the sometimes misunderstood hiss of a newly opened beer bottle. Audiences were quick, too, in voicing their approval or disapproval of the spectacle they were offered as entertainment. The price of admission was a penny or more at the Globe, and sixpence or more at the Blackfriars, at a time when the wage even of a skilled labourer might well be less than twelve pence daily. A large part of the audience was made up of the poorer citizens, and they were accustomed to insisting on value for their money. Audiences of more than two thousand people, which was the Globe's capacity, could insist very effectively.

Besides performing in their commercial theatres, the actors might be summoned several times a year to perform their plays at Court. Over the Christmas season particularly Queen Elizabeth would be likely to see a number of plays. Many of them were Shakespeare's. In the early years of King James Shakespeare's company acted at Court more often than all the other companies put together. The fee—£10 for each play performed—was a useful bonus, and the effort was slight. The actors would simply pick up their costumes and the few properties they needed after their afternoon performance, and take a boat upriver to perform by candlelight at whatever hall in the palace had been set aside for the occasion. It was possibly at one such occasion that Shakespeare met the mother who commissioned him to write the first of his sonnets to the young man.

The staging of the plays, then, was plain and fast. Some conventions were standard, such as scenes for the clown, and the poorer people speaking in prose while the educated and the noble spoke verse, but for the most part the acting and the staging were thoroughly realistic. Some actors were not only skilled at oratory but at sword-fighting. Duels on stage, such as Hamlet's with Laertes, or that of Coriolanus with Aufidius, would certainly have been spectacularly realistic. Costumes were often truly lavish. An aristocrat, having worn a suit of clothes once or twice, would give it to his servant who would sell it to the actors. Period costume such as Roman togas for the Senators in *Coriolanus* might be used, but the ordinary soldiers would wear Elizabethan armour and the citizens everyday London workman's dress. Because there was no fixed scenery, there was little attempt to localise scenes. A reference early in a scene to the market place or a house or the gates of Corioli would fix a locality where necessary. Otherwise there was little attempt to invoke the literal-minded realism which calls for each scene to be identified in space and time. The context of the play's action was enough. The scenes flowed continuously from beginning to end without a pause. Characters came on and went off with little concern for the apparent passage of days or distances. The illusion was never seriously projected as reality.

Roman history and politics

Nine of the plays Shakespeare wrote in the 1590s are about English government and society. In *King John* (1589?1595?) and the two sequences of plays dealing with English kings from Richard II to Henry VII he examined the three major political crises which raised questions about the nature of power and authority in government. In a monarchy where the ruler gained his title to rule by inheritance, and claimed God's authority for it, those occasions when a king's title was challenged and he was overthrown by a usurper illustrated most clearly the difficulties of such a form of government. Shakespeare's plays present all three of the crises when one claimant usurped the title of another. The English history plays are marvellously subtle and exact presentations, not just of what happened, but of how legal tangles and the interaction of different personalities could influence events for good or bad. Taken together they are an extraordinarily searching analysis of the political process in sixteenth-century England.

While he was writing the last play of the final series, *Henry V*, in the summer of 1599, Shakespeare started reading Roman history in preparation for a new series of political analyses. Roman history offered some distinct advantages over English history. Rome began as a monarchy, changed into a republic, and eventually returned to a monarchy, though it was one in which the new rulers—the first Caesars—took power by force of arms, not by legal title. *Julius Caesar* is set in Rome at the time when the republic was poised to turn back into a monarchy (the Empire). Those who compete in it for power do so in the interests of their own ambition rather than in the interests of law and justice. Brutus assassinates Caesar because he is afraid of Caesar's ambition to be king and because he values the constraints set on personal ambition by republican government. But Brutus himself dies in what is effectively a lost cause. Under the pressure of individuals lusting for power monarchy comes back to Rome, and Rome becomes an Empire. The advantage of such a series of events for Shakespeare was that it showed personal ambition, the interaction of political personalities, in an arena free from the constraints of English history. England had a body of law, and a law of succession which made the dynastic question of legal title to the crown central to any political analysis. It had the awkward theory of Divine Right, God's support for the law. Rome had no such governing principle. There men fought and manoeuvred with no principles, nothing but their own personalities to influence the issue.

Julius Caesar is the only play in this new series which Shakespeare completed. *Antony and Cleopatra*, which should have been the sequel, and which is heralded in the last two Acts of *Julius Caesar*, was written eight years later and reflects a quite different set of preoccupations from the questions of government and society which shaped *Henry V* and *Julius Caesar* in 1599. In different forms the two Roman plays demonstrate the transition from republic to empire. But in the eight years which intervened between them the focus changed. *Antony and Cleopatra* is a tragedy rather than a history, its central feature the lovers whose deaths mark only incidentally the beginning of Octavius Caesar's rule as the first Roman emperor. Tragedy puts more emphasis on the individual than on the social framework in which he exists. History, it seems, did not allow Shakespeare the scope he came to need for the study of man which he gave us in the great tragedies, *Hamlet* (1600), *Othello* (1603), *King Lear* (1605), *Macbeth* (1606) and *Antony and Cleopatra.*

Where does *Coriolanus* stand in this pattern of shifting preoccupations? It was written at about the same time as *Antony and Cleopatra*: either just before or just after, in about 1607. After these two Roman plays Shakespeare turned away forever from historical and tragic subjects, and began the series of romances, with *Pericles* (1607–8), *Cymbeline* (1609), *The Winter's Tale* (1610) and *The Tempest* (1610–11), which were the last plays to which he devoted himself. So *Coriolanus*, which is focused much more directly on political matters than *Antony and Cleopatra*, is Shakespeare's final presentation of a society and its government. It is set in the earliest days of Rome as a republic, when it was a small city state fighting for its life against the competing city states on the plains of Latium. Coriolanus himself is said to have fought in the struggle to expel the last of Rome's tyrannical kings. The two classes of Roman citizen, the noble patricians and the mass of plebeians, have joined together to remove the head of their state and in the play they struggle to cope with the political tensions which arise in a headless community.

In these respects *Coriolanus* shows the familiar preoccupations of the history plays deployed over new ground. The play is also, of course, and perhaps more emphatically, a tragedy. But the question of the balance between history and tragedy is one which belongs with critical analysis of the play's structure, not with the outline of Roman history and society which forms a background to the play and which is our immediate concern.

Elizabethan students of politics generally followed Aristotle (384–322BC) in his identification of three basic forms of government: monarchy, aristocracy and democracy. Students of the English constitution such as Sir Thomas Smith (1513–77) in *De Republica Anglorum* (1565) claimed that England had a mixed form of government, a 'monarchia temperata' or modified monarchy. Rome's republic was also a mixed form, a modified aristocracy. Constitutionally power and authority lay in the hands of the Senate, or council of patricians, the men of the aristocratic class. Executive authority lay in the hands of two consuls, who served for one year and then became ineligible for further service. They were nominated by the Senate from amongst their own membership, and elected by the votes of the plebeians. In time of war a single dictator might be appointed to hold authority for a maximum of six months. Quite early in the republic's life the plebeians demanded a more positive share in government, and were granted by the Senate the right to elect tribunes, or spokesmen, who had major powers of veto. The first creation of the post of tribune takes place in Act I of *Coriolanus*. Essentially the role of the patricians in government was positive. They created and authorised Rome's laws and provided its governors from amongst themselves. The role of the plebeians was negative, or at least defensive. They could block the passage of any decrees thought to be hostile to the citizens. The tribunes in *Coriolanus* specify their duty as defenders of citizen rights, 'the old prerogative' (III.3.14).

The constitution of the Roman republic was distinctive above all in its rejection of a single titular ruler. Monarchy was in one form or another almost the only form of government in all the countries of sixteenth-century Europe. A headless state was a rare and in many respects an abnormal thing in Shakespeare's day. When in the opening scene of the play Menenius tells the fable of the belly and the limbs of the body politic, he calls the Senate Rome's belly, and does not identify a head, even though the citizen to whom he tells the fable lists amongst the standard features of a body politic the 'kingly crowned head' (I.1.114). The republican Rome of *Coriolanus* was thus an object of curiosity for its non-monarchic government.

A note on the text

Coriolanus never appeared in print in Shakespeare's lifetime. The only edition with any authority is that in the First Folio edition produced as Shakespeare's memorial in 1623. All subsequent editions derive from that. It was placed first among the tragedies in that collection, although *Troilus and Cressida* was shifted in front of it rather late in the course of printing the Folio. The editors tried to arrange the histories and tragedies in the chronological order of their subjects, and evidently put *Coriolanus* there because it deals with the earliest historical period of all the plays.

The Folio text was printed fairly accurately so far as can be told in the absence of any more authoritative source. About forty words, a dozen attributions of speakers and some punctuation are thought by the most recent editors to have been inaccurately printed. The language of the play is generally curt, and metaphors are sometimes so compressed that their meaning is open to argument. A few distinctive spellings and the descriptive nature of the stage directions make it likely that the manuscript copy used by the Folio printers was the author's own. His handwriting was not always easy for the printers to follow, and this has licensed editors to conjecture misreadings in numerous places where the meaning of the printed text is not immediately clear. But the presence of fifty or so identifiable errors in a play of 3,400 lines does not suggest incompetent printers. The text is generally reliable.

It is desirable therefore to consult *Coriolanus* in an edition which has not received too much alteration at the hands of its editor. The old habit of giving the locale for each scene should be ignored. Where it matters the locale will be mentioned by one of the speakers near the beginning of the scene. Any text which fails to note the alterations its editor has made to the Folio original should be regarded cautiously. The best modern editions note all textual emendations along with their glosses of difficult words or phrases.

These notes use the New Arden edition, edited by Philip Brock-bank, Methuen, London, 1976, for all quotations and line references. See note on editions, Part 5, p.68.

Part 2

Summaries
of CORIOLANUS

A general summary

The problem before the rulers in Shakespeare's Roman plays was that they had come to power as generals rather than monarchs. *Coriolanus* shows this clearly, for the play can be divided broadly into three sections or movements. The first is primarily Rome at war, and displays Coriolanus's military prowess. The second is Rome at peace, and Coriolanus's inability to change the nature which is so successful in war to the diplomatic arts of government in peace. The third section shows the consequences of his inability, in the tragic movement to his death in exile.

The play opens with a riot. The Senate has been refusing to release its stock of corn, and the citizens are on the way to take it by force. They are chiefly aggrieved against Caius Martius, whom they see as the Senator most opposed to them. On their way they meet the old Senator Menenius, who holds them up with his fable of the belly until Martius himself arrives to quell the riot. He brings the news that the citizens have been granted tribunes to speak for them, much to his own disgust. Further confrontation however halts abruptly when news arrives that the neighbouring state of the Volsces is planning to attack Rome. The factions unite out of necessity to face the common enemy, and Martius leads the citizens in the capture of the Volscian city of Corioli. He accomplishes this almost single-handed, and to honour his victory is awarded the name Coriolanus. This action takes up the ten scenes of Act I.

In Acts II and III Coriolanus descends from the height of military triumph to solitary banishment. The Senate nominates him for the consulship, but the citizens and especially the newly appointed tribunes are wary of him. They know only too well the arrogance which is part and parcel of his heroism, and they have already witnessed his scorn of the unmilitant citizens. Nonetheless they are prepared to elect him consul if he will show a change of attitude. The price of the consulship, as one citizen tries to tell him, is only 'to ask it kindly' (II.3.75). But there is a fearsome ambiguity in that assertion. To be kind, humane, is a reasonable requirement in a governor. But Coriolanus's kind, his nature, is too arrogant. 'Would you have me/False to my nature?'

(III.2.14–15) he asks his mother, as she persuades him to humble his pride and ask the citizens for their votes. Twice he agrees to try, and both times he cannot suppress his nature. The anger which bursts out in the end produces a conflict within 'the body o' th' weal' (II.3.180) that threatens to make it 'cleave in the midst and perish' (III.2.28). Something has to be sacrificed to keep the city whole, and it must be Coriolanus, the chief cause of the cleavage. In time of peace it proves impossible to have a ruler like Coriolanus whose nature makes him show himself

> *commanding peace*
> *Even with the same austerity and garb*
> *As he controll'd the war*
>
> (IV.7.43–5).

Triumph for Coriolanus in time of war is followed by banishment in time of peace.

The third movement, in Acts IV and V, shows the consequences of the hero's banishment from his home. He leaves his family: his mother, wife, son and friends (Coriolanus has more close kin than any other of Shakespeare's heroes), to go off alone, nobody knows where. We learn that the Volsces, hearing of the Roman quarrels ('the people against the senators, patricians and nobles' IV.3.14–15), are preparing once again for war against Rome. Then Coriolanus reappears at the house of the Volscian general he had defeated at Corioli. His aim is revenge against the society which sent him into exile. '*I* banish *you*' he tells the Roman citizens (III.3.123). He will return to his victorious role as general in war, this time leading the Volsces against Rome. Aufidius, the Volscian general, accepts the proposition and they march out together in pursuit of their separate revenges. The pattern of Coriolanus's conquests and his downfall is now being repeated in reverse, amongst the Volsces.

The Romans panic. The talents of both patricians and plebeians, however much they may abuse each other, are for government in peace, not war. Only the arts of peaceful persuasion can stop Coriolanus from taking his revenge. So the Romans send their agents to beg him to go away. Coriolanus's former commanding officer goes first, followed by Menenius, who looks on Coriolanus as a stepson and who is complacently sure of his powers of persuasion. He, too, makes his attempt, and is rebuffed. Rome has denied Coriolanus's existence by banishing him, and he will prove he is not nothing by destroying it. But then his mother brings his family to him, the truly personal part of what Rome means to him. His mother, who had shaped his arrogant nature and taught him the honour of heroism in battle, had tried during the middle section of the play to reshape his nature for the political arts of peace without success. Now she tries to avert the consequences of her previous policy.

> Thou art my warrior:
> I holp to frame thee   (V.3.62–3)

she declares, and now she has to face the warrior destroying what made him,

> Making the mother, wife and child to see
> The son, the husband and the father, tearing
> His country's bowels out.
>   (V.3.101–3)

What was previously apparent in the body of Rome, the parts of the body fighting amongst themselves, is now concentrated in the one man. His different impulses are at war within himself.

Peace, of course, wins. Coriolanus turns away from Rome and goes back to the Volscian city, a man without a country. There the Volscians murder him for his betrayal of their cause, as he knew they would when he accepted his mother's plea and gave up his revenge. The tragedy of his death lies in the inevitability of the clash between his nature and the circumstances in which it has to work. The Volscian general, trying to explain why Rome banished him, offers three explanations:

> Whether 'twas pride,
> Which out of daily fortune ever taints
> The happy man; whether defect of judgement,
> To fail in the disposing of those chances
> Which he was lord of; or whether nature,
> Not to be other than one thing, not moving
> From the casque to the cushion, but commanding peace
> Even with the same austerity and garb
> As he controll'd the war; but one of these—
> As he hath spices of them all, not all,
> For I dare so far free him—made him fear'd,
> So hated, and so banish'd: but he has a merit
> To choke it in the utterance. So our virtues
> Lie in th'interpretation of the time:
>   (IV.7.37–50)

What was a virtue in war was a vice in peace, and the time altered its interpretation accordingly. Coriolanus is what he is. His names change as the times change, from Martius to Coriolanus, to consul, to traitor, and to nothing when Rome banishes him. But he cannot alter himself, to fit the different roles which the names signify. He is called on to be and do too many contradictory things, and dies as violently as he lived. The personality which brought him power cannot maintain it when the times change.

Detailed summaries

Act I Scene 1

The play begins with a mob of citizens rushing out on to the stage. They are dressed in workmen's clothes and carry wooden clubs and similar non-military weapons. They are rioting out of hunger, and hurrying towards the Capitol, where they might expect to find the Senators against whom their grievances are directed. As they arrive on stage they pause to rehearse their views. The First Citizen directs his grievances chiefly against Caius Martius (not yet called Coriolanus) on the grounds that he, of all the patricians, is the most hostile to the plebeians. The First Citizen identifies him as chiefly responsible for the Senate's refusal to release supplies of corn to the populace. The Second Citizen raises the question of the services Coriolanus has done for Rome, but the First Citizen dismisses them as motivated by pride and aimed at pleasing not his country but his mother.

As they are about to move on towards the Capitol they are checked by the arrival of Menenius, a Senator coming from the Capitol. His reputation is the opposite of Coriolanus's, of being an honest man who likes the plebeians, so they stop to listen to what he has to say. Speaking in measured patrician verse, in contrast to the gabbled prose of the citizens, Menenius denies the Senate's responsibility for 'this dearth' (line 66), or famine. He speaks calmly and patronisingly, openly claiming that the Senators care for the citizens 'like fathers' (line 76). The First Citizen, the spokesman and most vocal protester, objects to this claim on the grounds that the Senate has always favoured the rich against the poor in its lawmaking, whereupon Menenius tells the mob his fable about the belly. He tells it as if he were a father soothing his children with a bed-time story, although his motive for telling it is far from paternal, as becomes clear at the end.

The fable identifies the Senate in the body politic as the belly, and the outer limbs of the body as 'mutinous members' like the rioting citizens. The belly, says Menenius, is the body's storehouse, a word which reminds us of the First Citizen's grievance that the patricians have 'their storehouses crammed with grain' (line 80) yet are letting the citizens starve. Menenius claims that the duty of the belly is to issue its stores to all the rest of the body, keeping only 'the bran' (line 145) for itself. He does not admit, and the citizens do not get so far as to realise, that issuing its stores is precisely what the Senate is not doing, and what the citizens are rioting over. And at that point the citizens' attention is diverted from Menenius anyway, because the moment he has been waiting for now arrives. His metaphor now changes to one which more accurately indicates the true shape of his thinking. The citizens become not 'mutinous members' of the body politic but the 'rats' (line 161) who want to feed from the corn in the Senate's storehouse. Rome to him is not the citizens but the belly-storehouse alone. He has been conducting a delaying action until the city rat-catcher arrives.

He has been waiting for Coriolanus, confident that the young warrior's martial appearance will be enough on its own to disperse the rioting mob. As soon as he appears, Menenius changes his tone from fatherly patience to open contempt and abuse. Coriolanus too is openly con-temptuous of the citizens, on the grounds that they are cowardly in war and rebellious in peace, changeable in praising a man one minute and hating him the next. This is a clear reference to their attitude to him, whom they praise for his valour in war but hate for his scorn of them in time of peace. He scorns them for their failure to trust their governors the Senators.

Coriolanus in fact comes with the news that the rioters on the other side of the city have been dispersed with the promise (line 209) that they should have the power to elect five tribunes to represent their interests. He names two of them—the two we meet later—and dourly predicts a further power struggle as a result of their appointment. Angrily he orders the rioters home, just as more news arrives, this time a message for Coriolanus himself from the Capitol.

The message is of a threat of war, Coriolanus's favourite business. He sees war as health-giving. His concise image of how useful war against the Volsces will be is in fact taken from medicine. War is a health-giving 'means to vent/Our musty superfluity', which signifies the popular cure of blood-letting. It is an image of war as a means of letting out the stale blood of a body politic which Shakespeare had used before of the blood shed in rebellion, in the plays about the civil wars in English history. Health-giving or not, the first words of the Senator who comes in next, amongst a group of politicians, indicate how valuable to Rome are the military talents of Coriolanus. His nose for battle has warned him earlier than the men of peace, the Senators, that trouble is coming from Aufidius and the Volsces. Coriolanus is the obvious man to join Cominius the Consul in leading Rome to war against Aufidius.

The scene ends not with the march to war but with the two newly elected Tribunes discussing the tactics of peace. All the characters who appear in this opening scene are men of peace except for the martial Martius. The rioting citizens arm themselves only with wooden clubs, and when they are called to real war they steal away. Menenius and the other Senators are old men. Young Coriolanus thus recognisably stands alone amongst the men of peace even at the outset of the play. The hostile discussion of his character between the Tribunes which ends the scene underlines this point and emphasises the jealousies which attach themselves to fame. Coriolanus will get a name and fame through war. And the difficulties of maintaining it in peace are clearly indicated.

NOTES AND GLOSSARY

a verdict: a legal judgement made here in a situation far from judicial

rakes: the proverbial 'as thin as a rake'

a very dog to the commonalty: pitiless towards the people. Later (at line 161) the citizens are called 'rats', which makes the image of Coriolanus as a dog all the more appropriate

helms: steersmen of the ship of state

the bran: excrement, the indigestible part of corn

the weal o'th' common: commonweal or commonwealth, the term used by Elizabethans to translate the Latin *res publica* or republic

rascal: a physically weak or poorly developed deer who usually trails behind the herd

vulgar: popular

fragments: leftover scraps of a meal, parts of a dismembered carcase

vent/Our musty superfluity: make an opening to let out the stale excess, an image of blood-letting. 'Vent' and 'musty' also imply the selling of rotten corn

Act I Scene 2

The second scene brings in the rival general, Aufidius. He has the same understanding of Rome's military preparation as Coriolanus has of the Volsces, and the Volscian politicians are as reluctant to believe the worst as were the Romans. The powers of the two city-states are evenly balanced, each eager to possess as many outlying towns as they can. Rome at this point in history was in a very different position from its pre-eminence in the days of the Empire. It was one city-state among many, engaged in a continual struggle for power and even for survival. The least sign of internal troubles and its enemies would strike.

Aufidius makes it clear he has spies in Rome (we meet the news-bearing agent in Act IV, Scene 3) and is eager to take advantage of the famine, the riots and the hatred the people have for Coriolanus.

Act I Scene 3

We now move to the domestic level, and meet the mother of Coriolanus for whom the First Citizen reckoned he had performed his deeds of military heroism. The scene's primary function is to sketch the range of attitudes in the Roman matriarchy. Volumnia is wholly proud of her son's valour and his absence in pursuit of honour. His wife Virgilia takes the opposite view, frightened by the mention of blood, refusing to leave the house during her husband's absence even for the routine wifely duty of visiting a mother 'lying-in' with her new-born child (line 77). Her womanly pacificism is turned into a minority opinion by the arrival of the neighbour Valeria, who echoes Volumnia's militancy and praises Coriolanus's son for showing his father's violent temperament upon a butterfly. Coriolanus has been brought up in a thoroughly militant atmosphere. We are not invited to sympathise with one attitude against the other. All the women in their different ways confirm him in his temperament, his mother through the encouragement she has obviously lavished on him since his childhood, his wife by her timidity, offering an attitude easy to dismiss as ignorant squeamishness.

NOTES AND GLOSSARY

a more comfortable sort: a more cheerful expression

bound with oak: garlanded with a wreath of oak-leaves to acknowledge his prowess

task'd to mow: given the task of reaping a whole field of corn. Comparing the sword of a soldier on the battlefield with a harvester's sickle was commonplace

mammocked it: tore it into shreds, an idiomatic term

Act I Scene 4

This scene is the first of the seven scenes, the rest of Act I, directly concerned with the war between Rome and the Volsces, where Coriolanus displays his valour and is awarded the name we know him by. His outstanding bravery is shown in contrast to everyone, both his fellow

Romans, patricians and plebeians alike, and climactically against Aufidius himself. Although not officially general in charge of the Roman forces—as consul Cominius is the general, Coriolanus along with Titus Lartius only one of his lieutenants—he is emphatically the inspirational leader, single-mindedly determined to attack the enemy without hesitation.

The battle situation is outlined in a brief dialogue. Cominius with the main Roman forces confronts Aufidius and the army of the Volsces on an open battlefield near to the walls of Corioli (much as Aufidius had reckoned in Act I, Scene 2). Coriolanus with part of the Roman forces is facing the gates of Corioli itself, and keen to capture the city, so that his forces can then turn to assist Cominius. When the battle begins the Volsces, well prepared by Aufidius, charge out of their city gates and beat the Romans back. Coriolanus curses the cowardly citizens (probably the same faces we saw amongst the rioters at the opening of the play), and leads the counter-charge to the city gates. He pursues the Volsces into the city alone, and the gates (probably the main doors or the central opening in the wall at the rear of the stage) are shut behind him. Titus Lartius arrives in time to share the general assumption that Coriolanus will be killed inside the city, but the gates re-open to show a bleeding Coriolanus still fighting. The reanimated Romans charge in after him, and the stage is briefly emptied.

NOTES AND GLOSSARY

our fielded friends: our friends on the field of battle (as distinct from the besiegers)

cloven: split apart, cut down with a sword

against the wind a mile: Coriolanus regularly uses images of disease in the body politic. Here he claims the carcass stinks so badly it can spread disease even a mile upwind of it

carbuncle: a red solitaire gemstone, probably a ruby. The image is of a precious stone of unique value, isolated from everything else, and coloured like blood

---

Act I Scene 5

The citizens-turned-soldiers return through the gates of Corioli carrying their loot. Coriolanus follows, cursing them for their poverty-stricken mercenary attitudes. He himself is covered in blood (which he claims at I.8.9 is not his own) and carries nothing but his sword. The off-stage trumpet calls which were the standard form of battle-signal then call his attention to the main struggle in the open field between the forces of Cominius and Aufidius, and he rushes off to help, leaving Titus Lartius to secure the newly captured city.

NOTES AND GLOSSARY

movers: removal men, carriers of other people's baggage, paid by the hour

physical: medicinal, health-giving, an extension of Titus's calling the fight an 'exercise' at 15

Act I Scene 6

Cominius and his soldiers enter, in retreat. They are still under control, but defensively minded—'We shall be charg'd again,' warns Cominius. A messenger is just giving the cold news of the first setback for Coriolanus's forces (another Roman to provide a contrast with his valour) when the hero himself arrives. He wastes no time in urging an attack and setting off himself in search of Aufidius. A few violent words to the soldiers are enough to inspire them to follow him.

NOTES AND GLOSSARY

a tabor: a small drum used for dancing to, not the military drum heard along with the trumpet throughout the battle scenes

clip ye: embrace you

the common file: the ordinary infantry, now in military order but still unmilitary citizens

ostentation: display of intention

Act I Scene 7

Titus Lartius, having completed his arrangements for securing Corioli in Roman hands, sets off with as many men as he can for the main battlefield.

NOTES AND GLOSSARY

centuries: companies of 100 soldiers

Act I Scene 8

Coriolanus and Aufidius meet in the centre of the battle, with the trumpet-calls of battle sounding nearby. They fight toe to toe until some Volscian soldiers try to help Aufidius, when Coriolanus forces them all to retreat.

NOTES AND GLOSSARY

serpent:	snakes were generally feared and hated, partly under the stimulus of the story that Satan destroyed the Garden of Eden in his disguise as a snake
fame and envy:	Coriolanus' reputation and the envy it excites. Shakespeare's source emphasised the personal rivalry between the two warriors
Fix thy foot:	plant your foot so that you will not draw back
bragg'd progeny:	boasted race. Trojan Hector had a brother Aeneas who, after the destruction of Troy, was said to have founded Rome
In your condemned seconds:	through your misguided attempt to help me

Act I Scene 9

The Volscian trumpets sound a retreat, and the Roman leaders enter victorious. Coriolanus now has a bandage on one arm to signify that the blood in which he is covered is not all from the enemy. The wounds on his body, like the wounds in the body politic, have a central part to play in the drama still to come. Cominius as the Roman general gives lavish praise to Coriolanus as the chief instrument of victory, and when Titus Lartius joins in Coriolanus checks them quickly. Always curt and businesslike, he now turns positively surly under his friends' commendations. The more the Romans try to honour him, the more angry he grows. When Cominius offers him first choice of one tenth of all the treasure acquired in the battle, he refuses it on the grounds that it is too much like a payment or bribe for a service which should never be done for money. When the soldiers, who of course stand to gain by his refusal of such a large portion of the spoils, cheer him for his decision, he turns on them in a fury as men who shame the soldierly principles which they ought to stand for. They flatter him and therefore are liars, he says.

Cominius however will not allow him to pass as an ordinary soldier, and Cominius is not to be shouted at. For his service in the battle Cominius gives Coriolanus his new name, the first of several labels attached to him in the course of the play ('Martius', his first name, is the only one which really fits his character). He is assigned a role, an 'addition' (line 65) to his basic character, as victor at Corioli and military hero of Rome. All the Romans hail him by his new title. Name and fame are united. And his response is wholly dismissive. He is still covered in the blood of his achievements, so 'I will go wash'. In his own mind nothing has changed: he has done his duty, and praise is false flattery so he will not acknowledge it with so much as a blush. This is the first of a series of events in which his fame gives him a name and a role which he refuses to acknowledge without great persuasion. Fame leads him into role-playing which is contrary to his forthright nature.

The scene ends with a footnote which is both a revelation of Coriolanus's nature and a comment on the importance of names. A poor man of Corioli (in Shakespeare's source he is a wealthy man) prompts Coriolanus to a plea for charity. But when asked to identify the man he cannot recall his name. The battle has drained him, and his momentary humanity drains away too. Without a name, the man can receive no mercy. The incident begins a series of references to names, the chief of which relate to Coriolanus himself. His new name 'Coriolanus' marks his rise to fame, and his banishment without a name marks his fall. In society men need names. Names—whether the title just granted him by Cominius to acknowledge the fame of his actions, or the name which will save a kind old man from slavery—do not matter enough to Coriolanus.

NOTES AND GLOSSARY

against their hearts: the 'fusty' (stale) plebeians and the 'dull' (sulky) tribunes will make an admission contrary to their innermost feelings

caparison: the harness of a horse. Cominius makes this metaphor a literal truth at lines 60–2. Coriolanus affirms both at 69

a charter to extol her blood: as a mother she is entitled to praise her children

tent themselves: probe themselves (like festering wounds)

debile: weak

undercrest: to support like a crown or garland

Act I Scene 10

The first act ends with Aufidius, defeated and humiliated, swearing revenge on Coriolanus. He sees the battle not as a victory of the Romans against the Volsces but of the one Roman against himself. In his cursing he anticipates (line 26) the breach of hospitality by which he eventually will get his revenge. In a further anticipation of the final position of Coriolanus Aufidius finds himself cast out of the city he had tried to hold, aimless in the countryside near Corioli.

This scene is the last of the battle section of the play in which Coriolanus makes his name, the first 'addition' which signifies his military heroism. The incipient troubles which have divided Rome into quarrelling political factions have been suppressed so that the common enemy can be outfaced. But even during the fight against the Volsces we are reminded of Coriolanus's hatred of the people and their lack of military virtues. Now, with Coriolanus at the peak of his fame, we see him confronted with the consequences of his outlook in time of peace.

NOTES AND GLOSSARY

condition: ransom terms; more generally state of mind or body
city mills: that is, beyond the outskirts of the city. There were corn mills close to Shakespeare's Globe theatre in London, on the south bank of the River Thames

Act II Scene 1

Act I is the longest single act in the play. Acts II and III run together, and jointly cover more ground than Act I alone. They can accurately be thought of as the second act, or movement, which demonstrates Rome at peace after the display of Rome at war. In both Coriolanus is the central figure, but while he ends victorious in the first, he ends defeated and banished in the second. In the first, against his will he is given the name Coriolanus; in the second, he is forced to seek the name of consul.

Act II begins amongst the men of peace, the old men left in Rome while the soldiers are at war. It is not however very peaceful. Menenius and the Tribunes are at loggerheads, divided in their opinion of Martius (they still call him Martius because the news of the victory at Corioli has not yet reached Rome). Both the Tribunes and Menenius are magistrates, but neither side shows much sign of a judicious mind. Menenius speaks complacently of his failing in being inclined to give the verdict in favour of the first version he hears in every case. He enjoys his reputation as a man who loves the pleasures of life, and he enjoys mocking the Tribunes with his insults. The surface reason why they are at loggerheads is Coriolanus. The Tribunes see him as proud, which as we have seen in Act I, Scene 9 he certainly is not, and Menenius counters by declaring that the Tribunes are equally proud. Neither side in the argument gets anywhere near any sort of truth. Rome's magistrates are opinionated and obtuse. They are partisan, politically factional, out of motives which lie deeper than reason and which obscure rational judgement. The ninety-five lines of abuse they exchange—Menenius excited and verbose, the Tribunes surly—represent the characteristic attitude of each side to the opposition. It does credit to neither.

When the patrician ladies, the matrons of Rome, enter, the split between the two parties is made all the more clear. Menenius throws his hat up like a boy at the news of Coriolanus's success, overjoyed like Volumnia not at the victory for Rome but at the fame Coriolanus has won for himself. They gloat over his wounds as the physical mark of his prowess, and within a few lines Volumnia is thinking of the next triumph for her son. The scars will speak for him. 'There will be large cicatrices to show the people when he shall stand for his place' (line 146–8), she declares exultantly. The assumption is automatic: he is in line for the consulship, the highest rank a Roman could achieve. She and Menenius add up the number of his wounds as if they were votes.

In a manner which reminds us how contrary such thinking is to Coriolanus's own cast of mind, the formal procession for his triumph follows immediately. He enters crowned with the victor's garland, escorted by Cominius, the consul and general, chief magistrate for the present of all Rome, and by his fellow military leader, Titus Lartius. In the centre between these two figures, uncomfortably wearing the garland that goes with his new name, formally hailed by the official herald and greeted by the whole city amidst the shrilling of triumphant trumpets, Coriolanus stands unhappy and humiliated, the very opposite of proud. At the end of the ceremonial blasts he can stand it no longer—'No more of this; it does offend my heart./Pray now, no more'. When Cominius tactfully draws his attention to his mother he immediately makes the gesture of humility and kneels in front of her.

With that action Coriolanus turns from the formal ceremony of Rome's welcome to his family. To Volumnia he speaks one respectful but neutral sentence. She, in the emotion of her pride, stumbles in her speech of welcome and he is quickly diverted to his wife, to whom he speaks most warmly, in striking contrast to the formal greeting he offered his mother. He tries to joke her out of her tears, and in the same tone draws in Menenius—'And live you yet?' Laughter is the release for emotional stress in a family reunion.

Menenius in his joy makes the point that the family welcome ought to be all Rome's and yet is not. 'You are three', he says to the three leaders, 'That Rome should dote on' (lines 185–6). But some 'old crabtrees' will not be grafted on to the patrician family tree. The organic image he uses here, of the Tribunes as products of a sour or crabbed apple tree, grafted on to a healthy stock of patricians and yet still producing sour apples, shows yet again that his idea of Rome as essentially a patrician state, belonging to the aristocratic faction only, is habitual to him.

Coriolanus likewise reminds us that his idea of Rome is similar to

that of Menenius when he declares his intention of immediately report-
ing to the 'good patricians' of the Senate at the Capitol. Only one slight
discord affects the patrician family harmony. Volumnia produces a
heavy hint about the consulship—'only/There's one thing wanting'
(lines 198–9), which pulls Coriolanus up short. He has no such thought
of any further 'addition' to his honours. Warningly he tells her,

> *Know, good mother,*
> *I had rather be their servant in my way,*
> *Than sway with them in theirs.*   (lines 200–2)

He would prefer to be Rome's servant in war than govern with the
patricians using the arts of peace. He knows his own mind.

He goes off with the others, however, continuing the triumphant
procession to the Capitol. The old crabtrees, confirming Menenius's
jibe, remain behind to consider the implications of Volumnia's clear
intention to put Coriolanus up for consul. The lines of Rome's next
battle are being drawn. Brutus sourly acknowledges the hero's welcome
and the fame it shows Coriolanus has won. So much popular acclaim
is likely to get him elected 'on the sudden' (line 219) to the office of
consul, which would mean a year's impotence for the Tribunes. Sicinius
predicts hopefully that Coriolanus will prove too arrogant to last a
whole year in the same good repute with which he begins it—'He
cannot temperately transport his honours/From where he should begin
and end' (lines 222–3). They also take note of the attitude implied by
Coriolanus's response to his triumph and his mother. He thinks that
having to beg for votes and make the customary display of his wounds
is too high a price to pay for the consulship. In case the 'desire of the
nobles' persuades him to try, though, the Tribunes will remind the
people of his contempt for them ('suggest', line 243 and line 251, means
'put the thought in their minds'). His 'soaring insolence' (line 252) will
do the rest. The scene ends with confirmation of his nomination for the
consulship in the Senate as in their different ways both Volumnia and
the Tribunes had predicted.

NOTES AND GLOSSARY

the right hand file: a military term for the line of the bravest fighters

humorous: full of 'humours' or passions, not moderate and
balanced in mind or body

Lycurguses: wise rulers and law-givers, after Lycurgus of Sparta,
the legendary founder of the greatest of the ancient
Greek systems of law

ass in compound: their speeches are pompous, and like donkeys

the map of my microcosm: my face as the emblem of my self

bisson conspectuities: Menenius is baffling the Tribunes with sarcastic polysyllables. 'bisson' refers to old men's bleared eyesight, 'conspectuities' is a coinage from Latin meaning clearsightedness

mummers: the old style of actors, especially users of mime

giber ... bencher: mocker...magistrate or Senator

botcher: one who makes clothes from rags and patches

Deucalion: in Greek myth the survivor of the flood, like the biblical Noah; hence the first father of classical Greece and Rome

make a lip: sneer

Galen: the standard medical authority, a Roman doctor who lived in the second century AD

malkin: wench

flamens: priests, who rarely appeared in public

napless vesture: a garment worn threadbare, here deliberately put on to show humility, according to Roman custom

Act II Scene 2

The cushions which are now laid out on the stage mark the scene as the Senate house, the place of Roman government. Summing up Coriolanus's weaknesses, Aufidius in IV.7.43 says he would not move 'From th'casque to th'cushion', from the helmet of the soldier to the seat of the magistrate. Cushions are mentioned also in III.1.100 as senatorial seats. The officers lay them out in rows for the official assembly, gossiping as they do so about the prospects for the election which the assembly is to consider. Their gossip reiterates the point about faction and the mutual hostility between the two parts of the body politic which Coriolanus so strongly shares and intensifies. For the first time it is openly assumed that politicians commonly lie, flatter and pretend a love they do not have for the people in order to secure their votes. Neither officer expects Coriolanus to do so, and their conclusion that Coriolanus is 'a worthy man', stops short of saying that he ought to have the consulship. Their presentation of the situation is balanced, and more impartial than what follows.

Another procession now brings in the Senate and the attendant Tribunes, who sit apart from the patricians. Coriolanus stands while the others sit on their cushions. He is the candidate, there to be judged by the magistrates. The only business still on their agenda is what Menenius calls 'To gratify [reward] his noble service that/Hath thus stood for his country' (lines 40–1). Coriolanus is evidently standing before the Senate as arrogantly as he stood in front of his enemies at Corioli. We might remember here how reluctant he was then to take a reward for his 'noble service'. And yet here he is presenting himself for the reward of the consulship, quite as reluctant as ever, but evidently forced into it by his mother and his fellow patricians.

Cominius is called on to give the official account of the services which are to be rewarded. The Tribunes, present as the people's own magistrates, are invited to listen and advise the people accordingly. Sicinius gives a moderate and courteous response to that in formal terms, but Brutus, adding his word, gives an ominous warning which is too close to the heart of everyone's anxiety over Coriolanus to fit with the formal courtesies to which the Senate has so far listened. Menenius protests, and his brief exchange with Brutus shows the fragility of the attempt at compromise for which the Senators are hoping. Menenius is dismissive—'He loves your people,/But tie him not to be their bedfellow' (lines 64–5), a reservation which mocks the idea of honest love, and implies that feelings are mere words, the empty forms which a politician can bend to his purposes.

Cominius is a second time delayed from starting his speech when Coriolanus tries to leave. Brutus needles him, with a falsely solicitous enquiry whether his own warning about Coriolanus needing to value the people more kindly had upset him. Coriolanus is as blunt and brief in his reply as ever, and walks out, leaving his description of what is to follow—having his 'nothings monster'd' (line 77)—resounding in the theatre as Cominius begins the formal oration praising him. Menenius makes the best cover-up he can of this surly departure, and then at last Cominius, who has waited patiently through all the arguing, can begin.

The essence of Cominius's speech is that Coriolanus has demonstrated fully his possession since youth of the manliest of Roman virtues, valour. Thomas North (1535?–1601?) who translated Plutarch's *Lives* (AD66?) into English, and whose translation was Shakespeare's primary source for the play, explicitly made the point set out here by Cominius. 'In those days', wrote North, 'valiantness was honoured in Rome above all other virtues; which they called *Virtus* ... including in that general name all other special virtues besides.' In a world of small city states, each quite literally fighting for survival, bravery in battle was bound to be the most highly prized quality in a man. That was how the Senators were accustomed to view it, and on that basis Cominius nominates Coriolanus for Rome's highest reward, a consulship.

The Senators all agree, and summon him back to tell him their decision. He makes his customary brief reply, unimpressed by honours which represent fame and not actions. Fame is the 'addition' which follows valorous action. To Coriolanus the action is what matters, the true kind of honour, not the name and fame which follow and which the Senate have in mind when they 'honour' him. He accepts their addition to his name in the same terms he had used in his original reply when his mother first mentioned the consulship, that he serves Rome dutifully. With that blunt acceptance Menenius, putting it as neutrally as he can, next broaches the real problem. 'It then remains/That you do speak to the people' (lines 134–5). Coriolanus immediately begs to be excused from this, citing his objection to the custom of showing his wounds in public as a means of getting the necessary votes. It is a stumbling-block for which we have been well prepared. The noble blood which covered him in the battle in Act I has already been adulterated by Menenius and Volumnia, gleefully totting up the total of his scars (II.1.149–54) as the means to guarantee him the necessary votes for his next 'honour'. Coriolanus instinctively sees it as a deception, false role-playing like an actor. 'It is a part/That I shall blush in acting' (lines 144–5). The blush of his shame will replace the red of the blood which brought him to this deception. His valorous actions were performed for the sake of his inward honour, not his outward fame, and still less as a vote-catching device. To use them for such a purpose dishonours them. But the Senate demands its custom, and he is swept along by it.

NOTES AND GLOSSARY

waved: wavered, drifted

bonneted: removing one's hat was a sign of courtesy and respect. To put it back on, as described here, indicates that it is only a gesture, a pretence of respect made just for the occasion

defective for requital: not equipped to reward services adequately

nothings monster'd: unimportant actions inflated or exaggerated to an unnatural and improbable size

perpetual spoil: an endless massacre

Act II Scene 3

This scene is the climax of the mini-drama which takes place through Acts II and III. In a full tragedy there is a climax in Act III and a catastrophe in Act V. Here in the political arena at the centre of the play the climax is the attempt by Coriolanus to win the 'voices' of the people, the catastrophe its outcome in his banishment. Everything we have seen of Coriolanus up to now has prepared us for this crucial test.

We know how reluctantly he does it, how much exploiting the accidental scars of his fame to get an additional fame for which he has no ambition is contrary to his nature. Everyone in fact has acted in accordance with their nature up to now—Volumnia and Menenius pushing Coriolanus towards his ultimate 'honour', the Tribunes and citizens suspicious of the consequences and ready to act on their suspicions. What remains is to see the outcome of the ensuing clash.

The citizens who enter to open the scene are the same sort of men, if not the same men, who entered in the riot at the opening of the play. They do not have names, but are simply numbered in the order in which they speak. The First Citizen here, for instance, is clearly not the same man as the First Citizen of Act I, Scene 1. That man led the rioters and saw Coriolanus as the 'chief enemy to the people' (I.1.6–7). The citizen who speaks first in this scene is notably favourable to Coriolanus. He feels from the start that Coriolanus ought to be given their votes, and requires no more than that he should ask for them 'kindly' (line 75)—a rather tart response to the phrasing of Coriolanus's request for the 'price' of the consulship, but still a defensive reply, which more or less sums up the consensus of all the citizens at this point. They are uncomfortably aware of his contempt for them and his impatience over the customary ceremonies of vote-begging. All they want is a sign that his arrogance is blended with a touch of humanity. 'Kindly' is a double-edged word. To be kind is to be humane, but it also means to behave according to one's 'kind' or type. Coriolanus will do the one, but he cannot do the other.

The citizens take note that Coriolanus has already spoken of them as equivalent to headless—'the many-headed multitude' (lines 16–17). Elsewhere he confirms the reference to the monster Hydra (III.1.92), a beast with many poisonous mouths whose death, in Greek legend, was one of the labours of Hercules. Coriolanus clearly sees democracy as a dangerous monster. Many heads amount to no head. At III.1.145 he speaks of the citizens as an army commanded by 'general ignorance'. And in their discussion they seem partly to accept his judgement at least by the variety of their 'wits', as the third citizen affirms. There is some truth and justification in every partisan view voiced in the play.

The language and its rhythms in this scene are for the most part plain. There is some doubt among editors as to which lines should be prose and which verse, but for the most part the tone seems to dictate the rhythms as much as the social status of the speakers. The citizens speak in prose. Coriolanus speaks with Menenius in verse, but uses prose for the citizens in his early, stumbling attempts to match the 'gown of humility' he is wearing. At the end, the Tribunes, partly in passion and partly calculating, speak verse to one another. Prose is too plain, too ordinary for the intensity of that exchange. It is an ominous ending to the scene, heightened and made more portentous by the versification.

What actually happens in the course of the scene is largely predictable. Urged on by Menenius, Coriolanus accosts the citizens two or three at a time, and stumbles through his requests to them. He cannot dissemble without making sure his hearers know he is dissembling, so his voice turns sarcastic. He speaks openly of 'counterfeiting'—a standard term for acting—'since the wisdom of their choice is rather to have my hat than my heart' (lines 97–8). The reference in the previous scene to the flattering politician forgetting his humility as he puts his bonnet back on (II.2.27) shows how contemptuous Coriolanus feels towards the insincerity of the ceremony as it appears both in himself and in his hearers. When one citizen hints at the tradition of displaying wounds Coriolanus brushes him off—'I will not seal your knowledge with showing them' (line 107). He will use words as he has been shown they can be used, but will go no further, and will even undercut his words with open sarcasm. He is all too conscious of his 'wolvish togue' or 'wolvish tongue' (line 114), the Roman wolf in sheep's clothing. At the end of the agony Menenius re-enters to congratulate him: 'You have stood your limitation' (line 137), an ambiguous phrase since it means ostensibly the required length of time, but implies also that the constraint or limitation he was under not to fall into his natural manner has not been broken. With huge relief Coriolanus asks 'Is this done?' (line 140). The worst is over, and he has 'stood', or withstood, the strain of the limitation put on him. So he leaves for the Senate thinking it is all over, leaving the Tribunes to make sure it is not.

The concluding discussion between Tribunes and citizens shows that nothing has changed. The Tribunes still see his fault as pride (line 151), and act accordingly to shift the citizen's frame of mind. They work adroitly on the discomfort the citizens felt over Coriolanus's open sarcasm and his refusal to display his wounds. The citizens identify his scorn accurately enough, and under the prompting of the Tribunes come to see it as a more weighty feature of the man than his valorous actions. Brutus tells them off for not doing 'As you were lesson'd', or taught (line 175). The Tribunes are teachers, adroit at the dissembling arts of politics in time of peace. They can even make the citizens exonerate the Tribunes by claiming that the reversal of their original vote for Coriolanus has taken place in spite of the arguments put forward by the Tribunes in his support. Thus the Tribunes avoid the Senate's blame, and the emphatic nature of the reversed vote is affirmed.

NOTES AND GLOSSARY

voices: a resonant word for votes. It implies both vocal acclaim and the shallowness of words when used for political ends (like Menenius's 'love' at II.2.64)

a brace: a pair. The term was usually applied in hunting to a pair of shot birds tied together for ease of carrying. Coriolanus is hunting for voices

wolvish togue/tongue: the text is uncertain, but the reference is to a wolf dressed as a lamb. Compare II.1.6

the charters: Magna Carta, which England's King John was forced by his rebellious barons to sign in 1215, was regarded by Elizabethans as the charter of common law rights, the instrument of the people's 'liberty'

the rectorship of judgement: the controlling authority (correction or direction) of reason

portance: posture, attitude

Act III Scene 1

The events in this play follow one another with relentless speed. The situation is constantly shifting under the pressure of the conflicting attitudes. So we move from Coriolanus's plea for votes, through the reversal of the citizens' attitude to him, straight on into the confrontation between the patrician insistence that he be awarded the consulship and the plebeian refusal to grant it. The act begins with the Senators discussing foreign affairs, the routine business of government. They assume Coriolanus's election is decided, and that the Volscian situation is therefore the first priority. They are passing over the stage on their way to the forum, the city market place, to confirm what they take to be just the remaining formalities before Coriolanus takes the consulship. Titus Lartius has returned from settling the terms of peace, the 'composition' (line 3) with the Volsces, and they study his news. No other matters concern them.

When therefore the Tribunes block their path (on what for Coriolanus himself must be the supremely insulting grounds that it is 'dangerous' to go any further), the Senators are baffled and disconcerted. The Tribunes behave melodramatically, and one Senator is almost incredulous, insisting that the party be allowed on to the market place. The quickest and strongest reaction is from Coriolanus himself. He immediately interprets the change in the 'voices' (line 33) of the 'common mouth' (line 22) as confirmation of his view that they promote only anarchy. 'Suffer't, and live with such as cannot rule,/Nor ever will be rul'd' (lines 39–40), he declares, turning on his fellow patricians. He accuses the Tribunes of stirring the people against him, while Menenius hangs at his side begging for calm (lines 36 and 56). He is so incensed that he repeats his views about the danger of giving power to the people, using images of corn ('The cockle of rebellion', line 68) and of the body politic ('those measles', line 77) to describe how useless and damaging he considers the people to be. He rages on unstoppably. He ignores the attempts of Cominius and Menenius to silence him and renews his whole argument about the issue of corn to the people, the grievance which prompted the riot in Act II, Scene 1 and his conviction that the appointment of tribunes and the place in the government of Rome which it gave to the people was a wholly misconceived generosity, a 'dangerous lenity' (line 98). In his fury he is led on to an open plea to the Senate to abolish the law which established the Tribunes. Still using the body politic image he urges them to 'pluck out/The multitudinous tongue: let them not lick/The sweet which is their poison' (lines 154–6). The 'sweet' is the taste of power, what the Tribunes call the people's 'liberties'. A taste of power in the people will poison all Rome.

Such a plea might have been allowed in the earliest days. In the hearing of the Tribunes and under the present constitution, however, it is treason. He claims the Tribunes were appointed by force ('in a rebellion', line 165), not according to 'what is meet' (line 168) and in his view right, and that their appointment should be revoked. Their reply is to summon the aediles, a disciplinary force attached to the office of Tribune, to have Coriolanus arrested for treason. Sicinius in fact is so incensed that he tries to lay hands on Coriolanus himself. Coriolanus shakes him off ('Hence, old goat!' line 175), and a mob of citizens arrives in response to his cries. The patricians draw their swords, and a civil war is about to break out in the uproar. Menenius holds the violence off for a few moments while they consider the risk—'To unbuild the city and to lay all flat' (line 196), to which Sicinius replies 'What is the city but the people?' (line 197), an assertion which identifies the difference between the two parties. To the patricians Rome is property, what they hold. To the plebeians it is themselves. They all see the same object from different angles, and such agreement as they make is a compromise in the interests of their different views. Both sides accept law. When Menenius begs the Tribunes 'temperately to proceed' (line 217), he means 'proceed' in the sense of a process of law. It is by the law that Coriolanus is called traitor.

The atmosphere by now of course is too heated for temperate legal action. Brutus invokes Coriolanus's own favourite organic image of the body politic as the grounds for haste—'those cold ways,/That seem like prudent helps, are very poisonous/Where the disease is violent' (lines 218–20). And Coriolanus is indeed a violent disease. He draws his sword, and as he had done against the Volsces, he leads the patricians in sweeping Tribunes and plebeians off the stage. Afterwards the patricians are aghast. They use legal and organic metaphors together—'leave us to cure this cause' (heal this legal case, line 233), a Senator begs the sword-carrying surgeon Coriolanus. Cominius repeats his earlier reference to Rome as property, now a 'falling fabric' (line 245). Rome is collapsing about their ears, and the valour of Coriolanus is 'foolery' when it tries to outface tumbling masonry. Old Menenius is the optimist. His metaphor shows him clinging to the idea of an undivided body politic with no more than its clothing torn, which 'must be patch'd/With cloth of any colour' (line 251). All, however, are united in recognising the danger to Rome and the need to stop Coriolanus before his sword forces the cleavage in the body politic beyond the cure of words.

So Coriolanus is hustled off by his friends, and Menenius remains with other patricians to apply his patches. When the plebeians return Sicinius makes a point that was a commonplace of Roman law as it became codified in Renaissance Europe. Coriolanus 'hath resisted law,/And therefore law shall scorn him further trial' (lines 265–6). In the same legal language he accuses Menenius of resisting law by removing the culprit ('this rescue', line 274, is a technical term meaning stealing a prisoner out of custody). When Menenius begins to argue with him, though, he falls back on the organic image of Coriolanus as a diseased limb in need of amputation (lines 293–4). In the end Menenius wins time by reverting to the legal view. He will deliver Coriolanus 'Where he shall answer by a lawful form—/In peace' (lines 321–2). Since the alternative would undoubtedly involve bloodshed, the Tribunes have to agree. So the scene ends as do most in this play, with an immediate and pressing task ahead. The Senators have to alter Coriolanus's mind if Rome is to survive.

NOTES AND GLOSSARY

your herd: Menenius has previously (II.1.94–5) called the Tribunes herdsmen of 'the beastly plebeians'. His image then was of the citizens as passive beasts. Coriolanus here hints that the Tribunes are cowards (cow-herds) as well

palt'ring: being deliberately changeable

rank-scented meinie: stinking multitude, household servants

cockle: a noxious weed growing amongst corn

measles:	a disease producing skin blemishes (tetters); either the modern measles or leprosy
Triton:	a sea-god
Hydra:	the many-headed snake killed by Hercules
vail:	humble
th'rock Tarpeian:	a cliff in Rome from which criminals were thrown to their death
tent:	probe, drain (of a pus-filled sore)
tag:	rabble, possibly with a hint of raggedness which Menenius develops in his image at lines 250–1
cry havoc:	the final step in a war, the general's release to his troops so that they may start plundering and destroying what they have captured
clean kam:	thoroughly perverse
process:	legal steps, the due process of law

Act III Scene 2

This scene is in many respects a pivotal moment in the play. Although on the face of it what happens is a repetition—Coriolanus being persuaded to do what he finds repugnant and behave 'mildly' to the people—here the focus is on Volumnia as the persuader. She taught him his arrogance (even she called it 'pride' at lines 126 and 130), and now she joins the party of compromise, leaving him isolated in Rome and in his family. It becomes clear in this scene that if he does indeed prove 'dangerous' (line 71) to the safety of Rome he will be sacrificed.

Volumnia carries the weight of this implication. She enters to confront the still furious Coriolanus with all the arrogant authority she had originally taught her son. Her position is quite untenable. She has to argue that the 'honour' she taught him should give way to 'policy' (line 42), that he should indeed be 'false to my nature' (line 15), the question he first challenges her with. Such a reversal of outlook is of course no more than Menenius and the patricians have urged on Coriolanus already. For Volumnia to urge the same policy brings the inherent contradiction in the patrician outlook into the open, and serves as a measure of how much Coriolanus is truly a victim of the political circumstances of war and peace which bred him.

Coriolanus is forced now, as before, to agree to make the attempt. He directs his resentment now wholly against his mother for the unshrinking way she holds her untenable position. The more she pleads, using 'pray' and 'prithee' in a manner of speech hostile to her own nature, the more angrily Coriolanus responds. She puts her specious

case: 'I have heard you say,/Honour and policy, like unsever'd friends,/I'
th' war do grow together: grant that, and tell me,/In peace what each
of them by th'other lose/That they combine not there' (lines 41–5), to
which he can reply only with a scornful gesture. The model of conduct
she has taught him she now modifies: 'I would dissemble with my nature
where/My fortunes and my friends at stake requir'd/I should do so in
honour' (lines 62–4). 'Honour' now demands that he acts a part false
to his nature.

While he stands silent under this assault, Menenius and Cominius
join Volumnia in offering him a coaching lesson on how to act. 'Come,
come, we'll prompt you' (line 106), says Cominius. It is, says Menenius,
'Only fair speech' (line 96) they are asking of him. Menenius does not
value words except for their political usefulness. The people will pardon
Coriolanus 'as free/As words to little purpose' (lines 88–9), he assures
him. But it is still, says Coriolanus bitterly, a harlot's role they are
asking him to play. He cannot see honour in it. 'I will not do't,/Lest
I surcease to honour mine own truth,/And by my body's action [acting]
teach my mind/A most inherent baseness' (lines 120–3). Only when
Volumnia calls him proud does he change and agree to act the 'moun-
tebank' or swindler in order to gain the love 'Of all the trades in Rome'
(line 134). Volumnia has talked of policy honourable in peace as well
as in war. So he will pretend it is a war. Cominius the general has
ordered him to 'answer mildly' (line 139). So the password for the
patrician side in this new war must be, he sarcastically remarks, 'mildly'
(line 142). And of course like a soldier he will obey orders.

NOTES AND GLOSSARY

the wheel:	the rack, an instrument of torture
policy:	trickery, dissembling for a political motive
salve:	heal by applying a medicinal ointment
bussing:	coarsely kissing
action:	the gestures which go with speech in acting a part
make strong party:	strengthen your position on your side
unbard'd sconce:	unprotected scalp. The term is deliberately blunt and contemptuous
cog:	cheat, pretend in order to make a dishonest profit
invention:	a false accusation in law

Act III Scene 3

Coriolanus's second attempt to pretend, and to act contrary to his
nature, also presents a scene repeating what has in effect happened
before. The 'invention' or trumped-up accusation the Tribunes plan to

bring against him to make him lose his self-control is tyranny, his desire to assume the power of the kings he had helped to banish from Rome. It will provoke him into revealing his true feelings about the people.

The terms used by the Tribunes refer to the structure of Roman democracy, but are closely parallel to the English institutions of Shakespeare's own time. The practice of voting 'by poll' (line 9) and 'by tribes' (line 11), in electorates, was the basis for election to the English House of Commons. This emphasises the hint at line 14 when Sicinius refers to the 'right and strength o' th' commons' as a term meaning not just the common people and their common law rights but the authority of the representative body, the House of Commons. The 'old prerogative' hints at the authority of Parliament as the highest court of justice in the land and the chief defence for civil liberties. Constitutionally it was the primary safeguard against tyranny.

Events turn out exactly as the Tribunes hoped and the Senators feared. While Coriolanus thinks of himself as consul, and demands to know why the vote for him was reversed (lines 59–61), the Tribunes see him at the opposite end of the political scale and charge him with treason. Within his own view Coriolanus is right to call the Tribunes liars (line 73). He is utterly loyal to his idea of Rome. And within their view of Rome and its liberties the Tribunes are right too. Coriolanus has repeatedly declared in public his view that the constitution of Rome is wrong and that power should be returned to the exclusive control of the patricians. He denies the validity of the law under which he stands accused. If the law is Rome, that is indeed treachery.

The Tribunes maintain the pattern of legal proceedings. They judge him as lawless ('What you have seen him do ... Opposing laws with strokes', lines 78–80) and sentence him to the fate most appropriate under the legal view of things, banishment. Whereas in the body-politic image death would be the surgical means of removing him, under this legal view the Tribunes appropriately make him an outlaw. Coriolanus himself still thinks in terms of war, not justice. 'Have the power still/To banish your defenders' (lines 127–8), he warns them, and they will soon find themselves enslaved, 'Abated captives' (line 132). The law needs soldiers to defend it. And the implication is, slaves have no legal rights of any kind, no true place in any body politic. There is some truth, once again, in all these views.

NOTES AND GLOSSARY

the spoil got on the Antiates: the plunder at Corioli. Compare I.9.37–40
for the poorest piece/Will bear the knave by th'volume: for the smallest coin will suffer to be called a villain countless times

service:	Coriolanus thinks of military service; Brutus of legal or political
season'd office:	traditional practices
common cry of curs:	pack of scavenging dogs

Act IV Scene 1

What war has done for Coriolanus, peace has undone. The fourth act now turns from valour in war and the politics of peace to the question of what is left for Coriolanus in his isolation. Without a society or even a family he has no role to play. Honour and all the values he has been taught are now meaningless outside the society which gave them their point. He reminds his mother of all the precepts she taught him to harden his heart (lines 10–11), and present himself as 'a lonely dragon', a law to itself and a terror to the countryside. He reassures all his friends that he will continue to be himself—'you shall/Hear from me still, and never of me aught/But what is like me formerly' (lines 51–3)—but he can hardly know yet what the rules for a dragon's honour may be. So he departs, allowing nobody to accompany him further than the gate of the city, into the limbo of banishment and solitude, an unchartered voyager.

NOTES AND GLOSSARY

being gentle wounded: aristocrats must behave nobly even when wounded

My sometime general: Cominius, his former commander

cautelous baits:	the inhabitants of the country where a dragon lives will try to trap him like a beast with poisonous baits and tricks

Act IV Scene 2

The parties involved in the clash which sent Coriolanus into his dragon-like exile have to live together in Rome still. So we witness the Tribunes facing Volumnia's wrath, and the invective which continues to hold the two parties so far from each other. This scene is necessary to fill in the background of Rome during Coriolanus's banishment, and to push Volumnia nearer to the centre of attention. She has twice prevailed on Coriolanus, first to be a valiant soldier, and then to act the part of the politician, a man who loves the people. She has a third occasion for prevailing on him still to come, and consequently has to impress herself strongly on the audience in readiness for that final and most deadly occasion.

NOTES AND GLOSSARY

ancient:	traditional, customary. Compare IV.1.3
mankind:	male, a man (that is, unwomanly)
foxship:	the quality of ingratitude. It is a retort to the 'mankind' of line 16
in Arabia:	in the desert, not in Rome
noble knot:	the bond of nobility
faint puling:	feeble weeping, like a baby. Presumably addressing Virgilia, Volumnia is advocating anger as better than tears

Act IV Scene 3

After scenes of such high passion some relaxation is necessary. The principal actors are now replaced by two furtive and almost anonymous figures, the agents who exchange the news between Rome and the Volsces. In Act I we saw how well informed both sides were about their enemy's dispositions. Here we see the exchange of information taking place. In the process we learn how ready the Volscian forces are to resume the war against Rome.

The scene is ominous, not only in its one-way passage of news from Rome to the Volsces. In the standard image of civil war as a glowing fire easily fanned to a blaze (lines 20–6) it emphasises the weakness of Rome. More ominously still, though, in the readiness of Nicanor the Roman to betray his city's weakness to the Volsces it anticipates the betrayal by which Coriolanus allies himself to Aufidius, a change which he announces in the next scene.

NOTES AND GLOSSARY
intelligence: news, secret information

Act IV Scene 4

Coriolanus, who first appeared in Act I dressed as a soldier, then in Acts II and III dressed variously in the false 'vesture of humility' and the senatorial toga, now appears in the anonymous dress of the exile. Having set out with apparent aimlessness from the gates of Rome to be a solitary dragon, he has gone straight to the opposite extreme from Rome, the capital city of his former enemies, Antium. In a characteristically abrupt speech (lines 12–26) he gives his reasons. 'My birthplace hate I, and my love's upon/This enemy town' (lines 23–4). The only possible identity he can lay claim to any longer is through the kinship he has in enmity with Aufidius. Just as friends can become enemies, so perhaps can enemies become friends. Coriolanus comes to Aufidius in Antium not so much in search of revenge against Rome as in search of an identity. So powerful is his nature that he cannot bear the nothingness of exile. If he cannot be Rome's friend and Aufidius's enemy, he will be the reverse. The determination to revenge himself against Rome and its 'dastard nobles' which he voices in the next scene, a wholly new frame of mind from that in which he parted from the nobles at the gates of Rome, shows the impact of exile on his thinking.

NOTES AND GLOSSARY

double bosoms: two bosoms (one in each friend)

dissension of a doit: quarrel over a trivial sum of money

Act IV Scene 5

Unable to stand ignominious solitude, Coriolanus takes his life in his hands by presenting himself to Aufidius. In I.10.24–7 Aufidius had sworn to kill Coriolanus even if it were 'At home ... against the hospitable canon'. Now Coriolanus offers him the chance.

He does so with characteristic directness. After forcing his way past the household servants, despite his humble dress, he presents himself to Aufidius without a quaver. In a long speech (its source is in Plutarch's *Lives* which Thomas North (1531?–1601?) translated into English in 1595) he describes his situation. Only his name is left of all the services he did for Rome, the name which affirms how completely he has been the enemy of Aufidius and the Volsces. He condemns Rome completely, 'dastard nobles' (line 76) as well as the 'voice of slaves' (line 78) which banished him, and affirms that he wants revenge: 'in mere spite/To be full quit of those my banishers,/Stand I before thee here' (lines 83–5). So either Aufidius must take his revenge immediately on Coriolanus as he stands there, or help Coriolanus to his revenge against Rome. Exile has emptied him of all feeling but the spite for revenge. He is 'Longer to live most weary' (lines 95–6). In his arrogance he cannot beg. He does not ask Aufidius to grant him his revenge. He merely offers Aufidius the plain choice, kill him or accept an alliance against Rome.

Aufidius, swinging from one extreme of the love–hate bond to the other, embraces Coriolanus and in the classic pattern of friendship immediately gives him half of his possessions, that is, the command of half the Volscian army preparing to renew the war against Rome. The dearest enemy, the most intimate foe, becomes the closest friend the moment chance offers the choice of a reversal. Aufidius, of course, who has swung once, may swing again. But all for the moment is ominous harmony. Coriolanus will give a boost to the Volscian plans. Aufidius has intended, he says, to attack only the outlying areas around Rome—'prepar'd against your territories,/Though not for Rome itself' (lines 135–6). Now Coriolanus with his inside knowledge can tell them whether it would be better to assault the city itself.

The scene ends as it had begun, amongst the household servants. They discuss the fame of the two generals they have just seen together. Reluctant to downgrade their own master, they indicate their belief in Coriolanus's superiority. At the end they rejoice at the prospect of war as more exciting than peace. In a comment which echoes ironically the implication of the events in Rome, the first servant declares the paradox that peace makes men hate each other (line 236), and is answered with the explanation 'because they then less need one another' (lines 237–8).

NOTES AND GLOSSARY

service: a word which echoes throughout the play. The servant's use here contrasts with Coriolanus's in the last line of the previous scene. Compare III.3.83–4

go to the door: leave and stand outside, like a beggar

canopy: deliberately ambiguous. King's thrones were under canopies, but the sky is also commonly referred to as a canopy.

city of kites and crows: where the carrion birds live, a battlefield

Whoop'd: the noise of a jeering crowd; also a hunting cry

wreak: the verb for revenge, with a hint of reck meaning understanding, sympathy

Thy target from thy brawn: your shield from your muscles

a carbonado: a piece of roasting meat, scored and cut for better cooking

sowl: haul, a colloquial term

directitude: a meaningless word, though the servant intends it to mean 'in the inferior position'

They are rising: the guests are getting up from the table. It is time for the servants to rush back to their work

---

Act IV Scene 6

Back in Rome we meet the Tribunes complacently approving the present peace. Unlike the servants at Aufidius's house they like to see 'our tradesmen singing in their shops and going/About their functions friendly' (lines 8–9), rather than the riots of the past, which they claim the patricians would prefer. There is a case for war, made by the servants, and a case for peace, made by the Tribunes. Even Menenius is subdued: 'grown most kind/of late' (lines 11–12), says Sicinius rather patronisingly. All seems well. When the Tribunes repeat their charges against Coriolanus, including that of wanting tyranny, 'one sole throne' (line 32), Menenius merely says quietly 'I think not so'. The citizens are happy. The scene is almost a parody of civic harmony.

We know however what lies in store for Rome. We witness the first warnings being ignored by the complacent Tribunes despite Menenius's warning (lines 50–6) to pay good attention to them. Only when Cominius enters with confirmation and immediately blames the Tribunes does panic set in. Cominius repeats the image of Rome's buildings falling which he had used in III.1.202–5, though now he uses the possessive 'your' as if Rome belonged only to the Tribunes. Menenius echoes his bitter sarcasm. 'You have made good work' (Line 96) at your new trade of politics, he tells them. The patricians are torn between bitter joy at seeing the Tribunes' misdeeds about to be punished, and despair that they all must share in the punishment.

The essence of the situation is voiced by Menenius: 'We are all undone unless/The noble man have mercy' (lines 108–9). And there is no likelihood of that since everyone shares the blame for his banishment. The nobility of Coriolanus is not such as to offer mercy without good reason. There is panic in the streets, amongst plebeians and patricians alike, in a complete reversal of the initial harmony of the scene.

NOTES AND GLOSSARY

what talk you: why do you keep mentioning
melt the city leads: melt the lead roofs of the city houses
an auger's bore: the hole made by a wood-drill
coxcombs: the hood worn by a professional fool or jester

Act IV Scene 7

The motives which drive one personality are still not entirely obvious. Aufidius has been shown raging against his successive defeats at the hands of Coriolanus. He has been shown reversing his hatred and in an impulsive gesture giving half his authority over to his former enemy. We know that Coriolanus would receive such a gift as his due, and offer no friendship in return, and we know that such an impulsive gift, handed to a man arrogant enough to take it as if it were his automatic right, is likely to be regretted. Here, therefore, we see Aufidius having his second thoughts.

We might recall in this context what was snarlingly said about Coriolanus serving under Cominius in I.1.260–75. There the Tribunes, assuming that fame was his ambition, consider that 'a place below the first' is the most useful for that purpose. The general would bear the blame for things which went wrong, and half of the honours would be given to his second if things went well. 'Half all Cominius's honours are to Martius,/Though Martius earned them not' (I.1.272–3). This is manifestly unfair. Coriolanus is not after fame, and would never think of serving as second in command to his general for such a selfish reason. But the relationship which the Tribunes outline in Act I Scene 1 has distinct resemblances to the relationship between Coriolanus and himself which Aufidius ponders in Act IV, Scene 7. Aufidius is now effectively second to Coriolanus in the fight against Rome, and will use that position for his own advantage against his rival.

Aufidius hints mysteriously at errors Coriolanus has made which will bring either him or Aufidius down in the end. This so alarms his lieutenant that he thinks Aufidius means they will not capture Rome, but Aufidius does not mean that. He launches into his analysis of Coriolanus's personality, partly to explain what he means by saying Coriolanus has 'left undone' (line 24) something crucial, and partly to justify his prediction of a future crisis. Because of his distinctive nature Coriolanus has been banished from Rome, and his 'virtues' (line 49) are subject to circumstance. Virtue is subject to fame, which lies 'in th'interpretation of the time' (line 50). Power is at the mercy of fame. And so, rather cryptically, Aufidius both explains Coriolanus's banishment in the past and predicts his downfall in the future. Coriolanus is repeating amongst the Volsces the sequence of events in Rome.

The speech analysing Coriolanus is the most balanced and dispassionate of all the interpretations of Coriolanus voiced in the play. It is striking because it offers three distinct explanations of his fall: pride (line 37), mistaken judgement (line 39), and his unpliant nature (line 41). A mixture of these three, says Aufidius, brought about his banishment. Each of the three has implications for Elizabethan—and modern—ideas about tragedy and tragic heroes which will be considered later (see p.60) in this study of the play.

NOTES AND GLOSSARY

darken'd in this action: overshadowed on stage, eclipsed in the military campaign

sits down: lays siege

sovereignty of nature: the osprey was thought to be the king of seabirds. As a king, fish turned belly-up to him, waiting to be caught

carry his honours even: keep the burden of his fame well balanced on his shoulders

chair: the rostrum from which his fame is broadcast

Act V Scene 1

Aufidius concluded his cryptic analysis of Coriolanus with the prediction that because of the thing he 'hath left undone' the victory over Rome will leave him even more denuded than his banishment ('poor'st of all', line 57), and that once in that poorest condition he will be at Aufidius's mercy. That prediction is the most cryptic of all. Aufidius gives us no way of explaining his thinking. The first inkling does not come until we return to Rome in Act V and see the patricians and plebeians arguing over who will go to Coriolanus to beg for mercy.

The Romans enter in the middle of their argument. It is a packed, intricate scene—technically the most involved and masterly of all the scenes in the play—and needs careful unravelling. Coriolanus faces three pleas for mercy in all. This scene describes the failure of the first and the preparation of the second, while anticipating the third. In the first eight lines we learn from the truculent Menenius and the abashed Cominius that the attempt by Cominius to plead with Coriolanus has failed, and that the Tribunes are now begging Menenius to make an attempt. This gives Menenius a position of strength in Rome, and he exploits it to the full. He takes pleasure in emphasising to the Tribunes how fully the danger is their fault. He revels in the report of Coriolanus's cold answer to Cominius. He expects to go to Coriolanus himself, and he expects to be more successful than Cominius. So he offers a show of reluctance, to make the humiliation of the Tribunes more complete and his own eventual triumph the greater. As soon as he has made his announcement that he will go ('I'll undertake't./I think he'll hear me', lines 47–8), he complacently announces his plan to catch Coriolanus in a better mood, and sets off.

We, perhaps, know Coriolanus better than to expect that the persuasions of such a shallow and self-satisfied character will stop his revenge. If we are unsure, Cominius's gloomy certainty that Menenius will fail should make the point. In a marvellously compact image of Coriolanus—'I tell you, he does sit in gold, his eye/Red, as 'twould burn Rome' (lines 63–4) —Cominius indicates his recognition, clearer than Menenius's, of the hardness in Coriolanus. Cominius knows that there is only one hope of softening him. So even as old Menenius struts off to make the second plea for mercy, Cominius and the Tribunes together turn to Volumnia and Virgilia to set up the third plea.

Cominius is a far less petty-minded and vengeful man than Menenius. His mind is fixed on Rome, not his self-esteem. He does not abuse the Tribunes and is entirely ready to ally himself with them for the sake of Rome. His concern, free from all factional or personal interests, anticipates the outlook which will be required of Volumnia if she is to plead successfully with her son to save the city. His outlook also serves to re-emphasise the central features of the political analysis which underlies the play. Here he displays the resolution, the clarity of understanding and the foresight which might save Rome. It is an understanding which puts the whole city, the community, the buildings and the people, before the individual affections or loyalties which inspire Menenius. The same understanding must inspire Volumnia and Virgilia.

NOTES AND GLOSSARY

sometime his general: his former commanding officer, Cominius. Compare IV.1.23

knee/The way: approach on their knees, a mark of abasement which intensifies with the distance covered

coy'd: was reluctant or shy

wrack'd for: worked for/wrecked (in the name of Rome). Compare IV.5.86 'wreak'

to make coals cheap: by burning the city. Menenius also implies that the Tribunes have laboured to keep the price of such commodities as charcoal cheap for the people

minded: reminded, put in his mind

offer'd: attempted

smelt/Above the moon: could be smelled even in heaven. The corn image relates to the opening riot about the corn shortage, and to Coriolanus's own frequent images of corn with reference to the citizens

the instant army: the army we can make ready immediately

dieted to my request: fed well enough to put him in a mood to listen to my plea

---

Act V Scene 2

Shakespeare wastes no time displaying the truth of Cominius's prediction. The scene in which Coriolanus rebuffs Menenius follows closely on the announcement of the visit because we have no feeling of suspense about the outcome of this plea. The only pause is for Menenius to raise his pride still higher, in the arrogance of his exchange with the Volscian guards, before the inevitable fall. Menenius is grossly over-confident.

His speech is ornate and studied, the reference to Coriolanus's fire being quenched by the water of his 'father's tears' (line 71) too pat: they can hardly be real tears at this point. The soldiers who jeer him back to Rome after his rejection give him a brief moment to recover his dignity. Their insults draw from him a renewal of the talent for invective he showed against the plebeians of Rome. But he is crushed, and Coriolanus has made his point to the Volscian general and soldiers.

Coriolanus displays some significant uncertainties in this scene. He has prepared a letter for Menenius, as he had for Cominius, anticipating his visit and strengthening himself to resist it. He is, in a way, now acting a part in front of his Volscian audience. 'This man, Aufidius,/Was my beloved in Rome: yet thou behold'st' (lines 90–1), he declares. Aufidius is watching, waiting for him to weaken. His declaration is a denial of weakness, and at the same time an admission that the challenge to maintain his hard attitude is not an easy one. Aufidius is waiting for the effects of the 'one thing undone' to reveal themselves. It becomes increasingly clear what that thing is. His declaration in the first words of his rejection of Menenius, that 'Wife, mother, child, I know not' (line 80) is perilously close to being a defiant denial of the truth.

NOTES AND GLOSSARY

lots to blanks: something to nothing, a gambling term

My name: Menenius reveals a set of values based on name and fame in his boasts to the Volscian guards

my lover: my close friend. Compare line 87, 'for [because] I lov'd thee'

tumbled past the throw: a metaphor from bowls: sent his bowl too far

stamp'd the leasing: authorised a falsehood

factionary: partisan, active on behalf of one party

the utmost of your having: a resonant phrase; Menenius goes downhill from this point on. The guard is telling him he can go no further

Jack guardant: a common sentry, a jack in office

block: barrier, a stubborn fool

properly: on my personal account

shent: punished, given a telling-off

Act V Scene 3

Coriolanus, seeing his role as unrelenting vengefulness, still presses Aufidius to acknowledge his success in the role. He admits the difficulty of his role, of showing himself 'sourly' to Menenius, and also admits that he has made a concession by renewing the minimal offer sent to

Cominius (V.1.69). 'A very little/I have yielded to' (lines 16–17), he admits, but now no more. He is excusing himself, the wordiness of his speech betraying his discomfort. So he is just completing his declaration that he will hear no more Roman pleas when his family appear on stage to make the third plea.

This time Virgilia, the wife of few words, comes first, and Volumnia follows her, reversing the order of the meeting in Act II, Scene 1. Coriolanus knows his weakness and is finding his 'tyrannical' (line 43) role more and more unnatural. And his mother exploits his awareness of how unnatural it is. When he kneels dutifully in front of her, she dismisses the ceremony of kneeling for the parent's blessing with a histrionic gesture—'Oh, stand up blessed!' (line 52)—and even more histrionically she emphasises the unnaturalness of his stand by instead kneeling before him. She indicates the exemplars of Rome, the matron Valeria, Coriolanus's own son, and with Virgilia at her side makes them all kneel to him. Coriolanus is human and weak enough to beg her not to ask for the one thing he has sworn he will not grant. That is the trap inside which they have both shut themselves. Volumnia however will not let him avoid the confrontation. 'Yet we will ask,/[so] That if you fail in our request, the blame/May hang upon your hardness' (lines 89–91).

The force of Volumnia's personality is overwhelming. Her arguments are thoroughly irrational: she threatens that Coriolanus will march on Rome literally over her dead body. And as alternative to such an emotional threat she offers Coriolanus the chance to make peace, to 'reconcile' the two opposing forces (lines 135–40). She, who had raised Coriolanus for war and celebrated the honour he gained in war, now orders him to make peace. From her histrionic position on her knees she asks him for the blessing of peace, to hear both armies cry to him 'Be bless'd/For making up this peace!' (lines 139–40).

Volumnia does not see the appalling irony in her reversal here, but Coriolanus does. Even she in the end accuses him of pride (line 170). In a voice like that of Menenius, confidently wrongheaded and obtuse, she whips him with her sarcasm: 'This fellow had a Volscian to his mother' (line 178). She here identifies the reversed pattern, though she does not see its irony. She draws on the devices of emotional blackmail which a parent can so easily lay on a child. And Coriolanus, torn by too much understanding like any child in such a position, admits defeat and acknowledges the price of it. The stage direction, *'Holds her by the hand silent'* (line 183), is the one still moment in a play full of loud speech and hectic action. It is the moment of his defeat. Rome, as represented by its 'mechanics' (line 93), carries little weight with him.

Rome's patricians, as represented by Menenius, are equally authors of his banishment. Even the plea for Rome as a whole, represented by General Cominius, cannot move Coriolanus far enough to break the solitude of his nameless condition. In the end it is the name, the role, of son which breaks him. He weeps (Aufidius later, at V.6.101, calls him 'thou boy of tears'), and hastens to complete the formalities of his defeat. He promises to do exactly what his mother demands, 'frame convenient peace' (line 191), between Rome and the Volsces. Aufidius murmurs his threat to destroy Coriolanus by working on this conflict between 'thy mercy and thy honour' (line 200), and they depart, Coriolanus to take his last farewell of his family.

NOTES AND GLOSSARY

The general suit: the plea from the Romans collectively

Their latest refuge: 'their final scheme', though ambiguously also 'their most recent means of escape'

affection: emotion, the opposite of reason

I am out: I have utterly forgotten my role

denials: since he has already sworn never to grant such a plea, he cannot be said specifically to be denying Volumnia's and Virgilia's plea

our dear nurse: another image commonly used under Elizabeth I (1558–1603) was of the ruler as nurse of her people. Compare V.6.97

longs: belongs

convenient: reconciling both sides, bringing them together

Act V Scene 4

Menenius is now gloomily sure that if he could not bring mercy into Martius's heart (the Romans no longer call him Coriolanus) Volumnia will not be able to. So he cheers himself up by more taunting of Sicinius. They see Coriolanus as god-like in his authority, and so divorced from humanity in general. Once again the audience's news is ahead of the characters, so that we witness their predictions from a position which exposes the narrowness of their thinking.

Shakespeare also slips in with the first messenger's news the information that the plebeians are turning on their leaders for getting them into this danger. War can be as divisive in defeat as it was unifying in victory. The second messenger however brings the vital news, and the stage direction at line 49 signifies the huge noise of celebration throughout Rome, the reverse of Coriolanus's silence at V.3.183.

NOTES AND GLOSSARY

dragon: the final reference to Coriolanus's growth from man to monster comes ironically just after we have seen him reduced to a boy

engine: a heavy siege-machine (as 'battery', 21)

in his state: in his golden throne (compare V.1.63), as a 'thing' or idol to be worshipped

---

Act V Scene 5

This scene runs continuously with the preceding scene, to show the welcome for the Roman matrons who prevailed on Coriolanus (still called Martius) for mercy. The senator who speaks indicates yet another reversal: 'Unshout the noise that banish'd Martius' (line 4). But turning the clock back is a wish, not a possibility. This is the last we see of Rome, its matrons and its changeable people.

NOTES AND GLOSSARY

your tribes: this indicates that the senator is addressing the plebeians. Compare III.3.11

Act V Scene 6

After the crowds of celebrating Romans, the grim-faced Volscian general enters. Aufidius is now playing the part in the city of the Volsces which the Tribunes earlier played in Rome. Coriolanus is to appear before the people of Corioli to justify his conduct in the war against Rome. Aufidius plans to provoke him there just as the Tribunes provoked him in Rome, so that he will condemn himself through his own anger. The pattern is as consistent as Coriolanus himself.

First Aufidius repeats his grievances to his followers. He overstates his case, claiming that Coriolanus stooped to 'flattery' (line 23) of Aufidius's followers, out of the inevitable hostility provoked by jealousy and Coriolanus's tactless arrogance ('I seem'd his follower, not partner', line 39). It is emotion, not reason, that prompts his murderous intention, but he is careful to seek what justification he can. In the end only the culminating grievance, the retreat from Rome, is a crime grand enough to warrant murder.

Aufidius makes that point to the 'Lords of the City', the senators of Corioli. The first lord agrees. They can overlook Coriolanus's earlier faults, but this 'admits no excuse' (line 69). Nonetheless, the lords would make it a judicial matter. His case must be heard, just as the citizens of Rome had to hear his plea for their 'voices'. And Aufidius will not wait for that, any more than the Tribunes would leave judgement to the citizens. He interrupts the proceedings by accusing Coriolanus of the very thing the Tribunes flung at him, treachery. Aufidius's charge at lines 85–7 exactly echoes the charge brought by Sicinius at III.3.66–7. Coriolanus's reaction is equally violent, and fatal. Aufidius provokes him, by the accusation of treachery, by his refusal to admit the name of Coriolanus, and above all by the charge of weakness, that the martial god was reduced to a 'boy of tears.' Such a heated confrontation could not be brought back to a judicial hearing, and so despite the first lord's pleadings Coriolanus is hacked to pieces by the mob of Aufidius's followers.

Aufidius cools slowly. At first he tramples on the corpse, an act the opposite of the respectful kneeling in front of the standing figure which we have seen several times in the play. But then, appeased, he can concede the 'noble memory'. Once a man is dead, his 'fame' (line 124) is manageable.

NOTES AND GLOSSARY

the city: historically this scene happened in Antium, the capital of the Volsces. For dramatic purposes relating to Coriolanus's name, the city's grievances against him as their conqueror, and the symmetry of the two opposed cities, Shakespeare sets it in Corioli

joint-servant: joined in 'service' to the state. Twin rulers were called 'jointresses'. Aufidius is affirming the role of generals as servants not rulers

he wag'd me with his countenance: he paid me with patronising smiles

upon him: against him

women's rheum: women's tears. Compare line 93, 'certain drops of salt'. Aufidius implies that the tears of Volumnia and Virgilia swayed Coriolanus, though it is his tears which are most apparent in Act V, Scene 3

like a post: like a messenger

counterpoise a full third part: the Volscian spoils outweigh by a third the costs of the enterprise

unholy braggart: it was unchristian to boast. Aufidius has previously denied Coriolanus the status of god

owe you: threaten

a noble memory: a rich memorial to his nobility

Part 3

Commentary

Political questions

Coriolanus balances a human foreground against a political background. Shakespeare creates with marvellous assurance and comprehensiveness a balance between the individual and his society, between the different components in that society, between the society in peace and in war, between boyishness and godlike arrogance, between anger and tears—the list is endless. The most adequate metaphor to describe his creation would be an organic image, where every component is part of a living whole, like the body-politic image of society which he makes out so discreetly in the play to be inadequate as a metaphor of social man.

Critics have usually taken various parts and declared them to be the whole, thus automatically destroying the play's intricate pattern of counterbalancing parts. Probably no one critical view could ever succeed in describing all the balanced patterns adequately. So we find views identifying *Coriolanus* as a tragedy, as a history, even as a debate about politics, where the play can fairly be called all three things. We find views claiming that the patricians and aristocracy or monarchy are favoured against the democracy of the Tribunes, or alternatively that the citizens need their democratic rights protected against the tyranny of the patricians, where the reality is a Roman republic or 'mixed' form of government favouring neither monarchy, oligarchy nor democracy to the exclusion of the others. We find Coriolanus taken to be a true tragic hero—alone against the world, or else a 'nothing' who needs names to show him what roles he should play. We find critics who identify his pride as the cause of his downfall and critics who see him as not proud but utterly a victim of his circumstances. This list, too, is likely to be endless.

However, before we can start properly any consideration of the play and its hero, taken as some sort of whole, it is necessary to see in what ways the political aspects operate in the play. Some account has already been given in Part 1 (see p.14) of the general background of Roman history and politics, and of Shakespeare's interest in them as it is indicated by his other plays. It remains to see what part this background performs in the play.

The progress of the tragedy is marked by the recurrence of certain key words and concepts. Each time they recur we are reminded of their significance and given a measure of the play's progress since the previous occurrence of the word. 'Service', for instance, is mentioned twenty-one times in the course of the play, and 'servant' five times, each time with a resonance gained from the reiteration. Coriolanus serves the State of Rome according to his own code of honour. He is a servant, not a tyrant nor, in his own terms, the 'traitor' towards both of his masters, Rome and Corioli, which he is accused of being. He is a noble servant, of a state for which he has little regard. As a noble his service is that of a soldier. The trouble is that in the headless State of Republican Rome the soldier has real power. The leader in war has undue leadership also in peace. Rome, lacking a 'kingly crowned head' (I.1.114) to top its body politic, suffers from the inherent divisiveness of its 'members'. The State is not a unity within itself. Each class fights for itself, the patricians for their wealth in corn and buildings, the tradesmen-citizens for their 'liberties' and 'ancient rights'. They unite only over foreign policy, the necessary response to military attack from outside which threatens property and liberties alike. Both factions were also united against the tyranny of the ancient kings, and the plebeians especially continue to fear 'a power tyrannical' (III.3.65). Soldiers like Coriolanus must continue to 'serve' Rome and its laws and liberties, as servants not as tyrannical masters. But if the State is not a unity, if the ideas of what constitutes the State of Rome vary between one faction and another, the concept of service is likely to prove too delicate for the brutalities of the fluid political situation.

Coriolanus has been raised from childhood to live by the ideals of patrician nobility. These are, in effect, honourable conduct interpreted as requiring military valour in the service of the State. That is Coriolanus's noble 'nature'. He is the epitome of patrician Roman honour. He is young and has not yet learned how to disguise his arrogant 'honour' with words and acting. Older patricians like Menenius, who is quite as arrogant as he, quite as contemptuous of those who are not noble, are thoroughly accustomed to concealing their outlook in the longer-term interests of their class.

The arrogance which goes with valour in war of course is by nature tyrannical. In peace therefore it is an uncomfortable attribute, and when the state of peace embodies a situation very close to a power vacuum, a precarious balance of conflicting class interests, a tyrannical manner can all too easily be misinterpreted as an ambition for tyrannical power. The Roman republican ideal was Cincinnatus, the general who left his plough to command the armies of Rome in 458BC, and who, having done his duty, immediately returned to his plough. Coriolanus in V.3.43 asks Volumnia to 'forgive my tyranny,' but he means by that not the tyranny of political ambition but the arrogance of his sovereign nature. His pride is an arrogant, god-like nature, not the 'ambitious pride' of the generals who compete for power in Shakespeare's *Julius Caesar* and *Antony and Cleopatra*. 'Service' and 'pride' are both easily misunderstood when the seat of power is unoccupied and the class factions compete against each other in their separate interests.

Coriolanus, with his unchangeable nature, is the constant in the fluid situation of Roman politics. As the situation changes, so must he if he is to keep his balance, and he cannot. Up in war, hailed as the conquering hero, he is soon down in peace, banished into nameless exile. Each time the situation shifts he needs a different role to play. He starts as 'chief enemy to the people' (I.1.6–7). He becomes Coriolanus, valiant soldier-hero of all Rome. In peace he is pushed to become consul, then is called traitor, and ends the central movement of the play in exile, citizen of no state, man of no name or role. With the Volsces he repeats the pattern, from enemy to general, to peace-maker and traitor, to 'a kind of nothing' (V.1.13), and so to death. It is never Coriolanus who changes, only the names men call him. The political situation reacts on him to shape his tragedy.

Structure

In any Shakespearean play a great deal happens. Many events are crowded together in a basic pattern which does not vary greatly from one play to another. The details however are infinitely variable. *Coriolanus* follows the basic pattern of a five-act structure, with climax in Act III and a catastrophe in Act V, but with subordinate patterns which are markedly individual. The political pattern, for instance, involves the three movements already mentioned, war in Act I, peace in Acts II and III, and the onset of Coriolanus's personal tragedy in Acts IV and V. The personal pattern of Coriolanus's fortunes is different again. His rise and fall in Rome through Acts I–III is followed by an identical pattern of rise and fall with the Volsces in Acts IV and V. As part of these patterns of structure we find detailed parallels and contrasts, the repetition and development of key words and concepts, and a series of ironic reversals such as Volumnia's switch from teaching Coriolanus honour to advocating 'policy' (III.2.42).

The length of the scene-by-scene summary in this study is a measure of the intricacy of the play's plot and construction. Some indication of the various patterns will be found there. In this general comment, the most useful point to note is how much actually does happen in the course of the play, how rapidly and how unpredictably the situation changes, and yet how logically each new situation develops out of what has gone before. The play is a marvel of dramatic economy. There is no sub-plot. Nothing is irrelevant, everything is directly focused on the central story of constant Coriolanus and Rome's inconstant political and social situation.

Language

To match the economy of the play's structure, its language is plain and direct. The greatest linguistic flourishes come from Menenius when he is insulting the Tribunes. There is a violent directness of language, a direct address to the central issues, throughout.

Along with this directness goes the theme which can almost be called a mistrust of words. Menenius and Volumnia both try to persuade Coriolanus that in 'policy' he can use words which do not reflect his thoughts. To them, words need not reflect reality. Similarly the names which they offer Coriolanus as a consequence of his fame never fit him properly. He is as uncomfortable under the name 'Coriolanus' as he is under 'consul', or 'traitor', or 'boy of tears'. The reality rarely matches the names given to it. The politicians exploit words, twisting them for their own purposes, while Coriolanus is exploited by the words applied to him. Names refer to attributes—Coriolanus as valiant, god-like, boy-like, proud, traitorous—all of which have some application to the reality, but never enough for the whole truth. For all the plain, direct language, we need to listen carefully and sift the words to get at the truth.

Some words are used thematically. The corn which is the cause of the initial dispute between patricians and plebeians becomes an image which recurs in several forms through the play. In battle it is the harvest reaped by the conquering soldier. In peace it is the wealth of Rome growing mouldy because left in store. When Coriolanus turns his sickle on Rome Volumnia warns him he will reap a reputation—a name—which will be 'dogg'd with curses' (V.3.144). She puts together the corn image and the name theme in this speech, turning Coriolanus's own images against him in yet another of the play's ironic reversals.

The most pervasive thematic image, of course, is of Rome as a body politic. The state as an organism is a metaphor exploited by the politicians, from Menenius with his belly fable to Volumnia who charges her son with 'tearing/His country's bowels out' (V.3.102–3). Coriolanus talks of curing its sickness with blood-letting, the Tribunes of cutting out its infected parts with surgery. None of them seem to admit the inadequacy of such a metaphor in a republic with no head, governed by an inconsistent alliance of classes with recognisably different interests.

Tragedy

In his analysis of Coriolanus and his banishment from Rome (IV.7.35–55) Aufidius suggests that he was driven out by a combination (or balance) of three things. The first he identifies as pride, the word which almost everyone in the play uses of Coriolanus's conduct. The second is 'defect of judgement', and the third his militant nature, trying to 'command peace' in the same way as he commanded war.

All three of these causes of Coriolanus's downfall bear a striking relationship to standard ideas of tragedy. In the many plays written to teach Christian morality in the century before Shakespeare, the so-called 'moralities', a man's pride was a sin against God and led inevitably to his downfall. The wheel of Fortune carried a man up to the heights of material success, and carried him inevitably down to the depths of deprivation and death. Coriolanus follows this pattern, from the triumph of his conquests at the end of Act I to the 'nothing' of his banishment at the end of Act III, the pattern which is then repeated amongst the Volsces in Acts IV and V. In Christian morality the great always fall through pride.

In the classical view of tragedy, as codified by Aristotle in the *Poetics*, his book which described Greek tragedy, a great man falls through his *hamartia*, his error of judgement or mistake, which leads to the discovery of his error, the *peripeteia*, and the reversal of his course, the *anagnorisis*, leading in the end to the purgation of his error, the *catharsis*, which both hero and audience undergo as a form of purgation at the end of the play. Aufidius hints that this classical pattern, too, like the Christian pattern of tragic pride, can be seen in the story of Coriolanus.

The third tragic pattern outlined by Aufidius corresponds most neatly with the modern idea of tragedy, and especially the modern view of Shakespearean tragedy. By this view Coriolanus was a man trapped through circumstance, a victim of his own nature. His personality being exclusively conditioned for war, trained to respect valour, he holds in an extreme form all the attitudes implicit in the patrician or 'noble' way of life. He scorns 'tradesmen', 'mechanics', and citizens because they do not share his values and aspire to his militant code. His outlook is that of Menenius, who talks of the patricians and plebeians as 'Rome and her rats' (I.1.161), the plebeians being the rats who are after the patricians' store of corn. Volumnia taught the same attitude to Coriolanus. But Menenius is perfectly ready to conceal his hostility in the interests of the state, and Volumnia reverses her attitude in the interests of raising Coriolanus one step of fame higher, to the consulship. Coriolanus is too extreme, too unbalanced, unable to 'carry his honours even', as Aufidius puts it (IV.7.37). In this way, inflexibly honourable according to his nature and his code, he is trapped by the changing circumstances of his time.

There is some support for all of these patterns in the play itself. The pride of which Coriolanus is accused at every turn is clearly denied in I.9.66, when his reply to the acclaim of the soldiers is 'I will go wash'. It is not ambitious or vainglorious pride which makes him spurn the fame and the rewards of his actions. And yet he is regularly charged with it as his prime fault. The accusation is a characteristic half-truth, or perhaps a one-third truth as the explanation of his tragedy. Similarly the Aristotelian pattern of misjudgement can be identified in his obedience to his peers and his mother in standing for the consulship, and in the loss of a role through his exile which led him to the reversal of seeking a new role amongst the Volsces. Aufidius hints at an error of judgement in the thing 'left undone' (IV.7.24) which will destroy him. And for the third tragic pattern, his constant nature in a set of wholly inconstant circumstances is always apparent. *Coriolanus* is a superbly balanced play.

Stage history

Shakespeare's play has been revived and adapted on many political occasions and in many political disguises. Coriolanus has been variously presented as a dignified patriot sacrificing his life for his country, and as a rough unvarnished soldier. Volumnia has been variously made the focus as a model heroic Roman matron, or as a domineering mother. In the twentieth century more than one production caused political riots. In Paris in 1933–4 a royalist production led to fascist riots. In Moscow in 1935 Coriolanus was shown as the betrayer of the people. In Occupied Germany after World War II it was banned by the American authorities for some years, since Hitler before the war had been openly identified as a Coriolanus mistreated by his people. Berthold Brecht (1898–1956) was preparing a socialist version for his Berliner Ensemble when he died.

The utilisation of Shakespeare's play in such diverse ways is a testimony to its complex and potent story, and above all to the balance of its presentation.

Part 4

Hints for study

An outline of a study plan

The chief subjects to study in *Coriolanus* are:

  (*i*) the balance between history (political) and tragedy (individual)
 (*ii*) the details of Roman government
(*iii*) the portrayal of patricians and plebeians as political factions
 (*iv*) the personality of Coriolanus
  (*v*) the conflict between honour and policy
 (*vi*) Volumnia and the Roman family
(*vii*) the succession of structural parallels and reversals
(*viii*) recurrent words
 (*ix*) recurrent images

The main words and images to trace are those relating to the State as a body, and to the Roman ideals of honour and service. Specific words or images to identify include

  (*i*) the body
 (*ii*) disease and surgery
(*iii*) service
 (*iv*) the 'addition' of name and fame to Coriolanus
  (*v*) references to acting a part
 (*vi*) animal references to Coriolanus (he grows from dog to wolf to dragon)
(*vii*) images of Coriolanus as red
(*viii*) references to corn
 (*ix*) legal terms

The play spares little time for description or establishing moods. It has no sub-plot, no comedy, no romantic interest. Only what is narrowly relevant to Coriolanus and to Rome in war and peace is offered us. Structurally therefore the plot is linear, a strict succession of events.

Notice too how the succession is complicated at regular intervals by a kind of overlap, where a scene revealing a new development is followed by another where the characters begin in ignorance of the new development. You should also observe the ways in which we are reminded that Coriolanus does not change while everyone around him shifts their position.

Above all, read the play keeping in mind that balance is the essence of Shakespeare's presentation of a thoroughly fluid situation. Few statements can be taken at face value, but few statements are wholly lacking in truth. The world changes constantly so that the balance of things shifts constantly. Note how every character except Coriolanus himself manages to adjust his balance to match the changes. There are three statements, at II.1.222, II.2.16–23 and IV.7.37, about his inability to keep his balance.

Specimen questions and answers

There are at least four main subject-areas from which useful questions about *Coriolanus* can be drawn. They include:

   (*i*) the personality of Coriolanus

   (*ii*) the political situation of Rome

   (*iii*) honour and policy

   (*iv*) role-playing

These are the broad subjects. In addition there are many matters of detail, especially in the play's structure and language, which reward careful study.

Here are four questions, and specimen answers, from each of the main subject-areas.

Is Coriolanus proud?

The citizens, the Tribunes, the Senate officers, Volumnia, and Aufidius all charge Coriolanus with pride. For the plebeians it is the main cause of his hatred of them. For Volumnia it causes the stubborn sense of his honour which will not stoop to 'policy'. For Aufidius it is one of the three causes of his banishment from Rome. The question is obviously one which Shakespeare forces on us, and is central to our understanding why the events of the play follow the course they do.

Pride was a key term in Elizabethan thought. In a Christian context it was the chief of all the cardinal sins. 'Pride goes before a fall' was the commonest of proverbs, and the standard 'wheel of fortune' idea of tragedy followed the pattern in which a man raises himself through material prosperity to a height of pride, and is then humbled by a fall to poverty and perhaps death. The fall which follows pride is a process of learning Christian humility.

If Coriolanus is proud, therefore, he must be viewed in Christian terms as a man ripe for punishment and the lesson of humiliation. However, the play does not follow such a simple pattern. When Coriolanus is offered the rewards of his valour in Act I, Scene 9 and Act II, Scene 1 he angrily rejects them. He refuses the spoils of war on the grounds that his service is degraded by payment (I.9.37–40). He resents the fame which Rome accords him for his service in the wars (II.1.167–8). He does not want the further honour of the consulship (II.1.200–2), and only accepts it with reluctance (II.2.133–4). His subsequent fury when the Tribunes and people try to withhold it from him arises much more out of his humiliation at having had to beg for it, and from his basic resentment that the 'mutable, rank-scented meinie' (III.1.65) should have any voice in the government of Rome, than out of thwarted ambition.

If what holds Coriolanus upright in the central Acts of the play is pride, it is certainly not ambitious pride. His pride is a natural arrogance which refuses to stoop to flattery, which scorns men who are less 'noble' than himself and who are not attached to the ideals of honour and valour, and which turns in fury against the city when it first embarrasses him with honours which are mere names, and then tries to strip those names from him and make him the 'nothing' of a banished exile. He never seeks the name and 'addition' which the city thrusts on him in return for his 'service' in the wars, so he can see no reason why the citizens should take the same addition away when he confirms his own constant attitude to it and them. The accusations of pride reveal as much about the characters who make the accusations as they reveal about Coriolanus himself.

What are the political aims of the two factions in Rome?

The plebeians whom we meet first in the play are complaining of hunger and exploitation by the patricians. 'Suffer us to famish, and their storehouses crammed with grain; make edicts for usury, to support usurers; repeal daily any wholesome act established against the rich, and provide more piercing statutes daily, to chain up and restrain the poor' (I.1.79–84). In Act IV, Scene 6 when 'the world goes well' (line 4), the citizens are happier (line 27), and 'Our tradesmen singing in their shops and going/About their function friendly' (lines 8–9). The Tribunes defend the 'old prerogative' of the citizens (III.3.17), 'Your liberties and the charters that you bear/I'th' body of the weal' (II.3.178–9). They are the magistrates who guard the law which guarantees the freedom of the poor from oppression and exploitation by the rich.

The patricians are also guardians of the law which keeps the city together. Coriolanus tells the citizens that the Senate 'keep you in awe, which else/Would feed on one another' (I.1.186–7). The nobles provide the controlling force which the 'many-headed multitude' (II.3.16) is incapable of establishing for itself. 'No public benefit which you receive/But it proceeds or comes from them to you', Menenius tells the rioters (I.1.151–2). The nobles consider democracy too many-headed to have a constant voice or policy for government. Experience, skill with shallow words of the kind Menenius is fond of displaying, and a direct interest in preserving Rome's material prosperity, its storehouses of corn and its buildings, are the chief qualities of the patrician faction.

Amongst their qualities of leadership they of course provide generalship in war. The greatest Roman virtue as the patricians see it is valour. Without success in foreign policy, which in those circumstances simply meant war, no state could survive. Training its patrician youth in valour was a primary necessity for Rome. Coriolanus is an extreme example of the patrician virtues, and an essential element in its survival. The Rome which became the greatest empire in the world, and which gave its law as a foundation for the history of the Western world, depended for its existence when young on the qualities of a Coriolanus.

The Rome of the play is a vital but intangible thing. To the plebeians it is themselves as the mass of citizens. To the patricians it is themselves and their property. Menenius sees Rome as a storehouse infested by citizen rats (I.1.161). Cominius sees it as a structure of noble buildings (III.1.202–5 and 245). They see it also, like Volumnia, as family, a tightly bonded unit of common values and interests. The citizens are not part of the noble family, and therefore whenever possible are to be rejected, insulted, shown their ignoble status and their low place in the state. All the Romans at different times describe the city as a single organism, indivisible. If the factions fall out the state will 'cleave in the midst and perish' (III.2.28). The pull of these contrary interests creates a continual tension, a risk of imbalance of which all are aware. The organic unity of the state is a myth, a hope of unity. The reality is a tense and precarious balance between conflicting forces, in which Coriolanus himself is the uncontrollable force which threatens to destroy the balance. In the end the need for balance destroys him.

How do honour and policy come into conflict in 'Coriolanus'?

When the unbending hostility of Coriolanus to the 'herd' of citizens threatens the unity of the State, all the patricians automatically put their interests in its preservation ahead of the honour of Coriolanus. As Menenius says, 'The violent fit o'th'time craves it as physic [medicine]/For the whole [healthy] state' (III.2.33–4), that he should 'thus stoop to th'herd' (line 32). If the State is to remain healthy, Coriolanus must offer the medicine of his humility. The honour in which Volumnia trained Coriolanus demands one form of conduct. Policy demands another. As she tells him, 'I have a heart as little apt as yours,/But yet a brain that leads my use of anger/To better vantage' (lines 29–31). Cunning, the 'policy' which seeks an advantage by indirect means, she argues, is useful in peace and war alike.

All Coriolanus has to do is to lie. Flattery is mentioned eight times in Acts II and III as an instrument of policy. Coriolanus is known to hate 'the suppliants for the people' as 'time-pleasers, flatterers, foes to nobleness' (III.1.43–4), but he has to give in to the persuasions of the other nobles and try it in the interests of the State's unity. Twice he is persuaded to act a false part, to lie and flatter the people, first at II.3.95, and more emphatically still on the second occasion: 'I'll return consul,/Or never trust to what my tongue can do/I'th'way of flattery further' (III.2.135–7). That has an ominously false ring about it, and is of course all too quickly given the lie. He is actually unable to pretend to be or even to say what he is not. The casual exploitation of words is second nature to Menenius—'Only fair speech' (IV.2.95) he begs from Coriolanus—and he cannot understand what Coriolanus finds difficult about producing them. It is appropriate that his confidence in mere words receives its setback when he tries to persuade Coriolanus to forget his revenge in Act V, Scene 2 and is rebuffed.

Honour is here represented as the virtue of war, and policy as the necessary virtue of peace. War is a matter of confrontation between enemies, peace a matter of diplomacy and compromise amongst friends. Honour leads to confrontation, policy avoids it. But that is an oversimplification, as Volumnia points out. When she tries to persuade Coriolanus to adapt himself to the policies of peace, she argues from his practice in war. 'I have heard you say,/Honour and policy, like unsever'd friends,/I'th'war do grow together' (III.2.41–3). If war in practice combines honour and policy, why not peace? The implication is that not the means but the ends are the essential consideration. Volumnia and the others are incapable of accepting the situation. They see the fame of Coriolanus leading naturally to the name of consul. They see the flattery of 'policy' as an unimportant means to this end; later they see it as a vital means of holding the state together. What they do not see is that Coriolanus is incapable of adopting those means because his ends are different from theirs. They see the name and fame of consul as the end; he sees his honour as the end, the name as merely an 'addition'. The means they demand of him are contrary to his own end.

What is the significance of the references to acting a part in *Coriolanus*?

Coriolanus suffers under all the names which are thrust on him. He sees himself as constant, dutifully doing his 'service' for his country and resenting all the fuss made of his achievements. He resents the fame he is accorded at Corioli, the attempt to reward him financially and the name which is thrust on him to celebrate his exploits there. He accepts with equal resentment the further honour which his patrician family then thrusts on him, the consulship. Only under their unanimous pressure does he consent to follow the 'custom' of asking for votes. When the people change their minds he resents still more the humiliation he has undergone. His subsequent attempts to act the part rebound on him and he is awarded the new name of 'traitor'. So, losing all the names given him under the changing circumstances of Rome, he goes as 'nothing' to Aufidius and begins the unhappy cycle of role-playing over again.

There are two sides to the question of Coriolanus acting a part false to his nature. One is the reduction of his 'honour' to the level of flattery and trickery with words, which is characteristic of Menenius. His inability to do this affirms his nobility. The other side, though, is the danger of such inflexibility in any man forced by his abilities into a position of political eminence. By his intransigence Coriolanus brings his city and his family to the brink of extinction. There is a profound sense in which man in society is always forced into playing a role: as soldier, as politician, as husband and father, and the failure to adapt between one role and another is a form of self-indulgence, of egocentricity, which can be dangerous for the society. Coriolanus cannot act as a soldier when he is in a political role, any more than he can act as a dutiful son when he is in the role of nameless soldier. The one is as disastrous to him as the other. By acting as a soldier when political diplomacy is needed, he loses everything and is forced into exile. By acting as a dutiful son when the role of a ruthless soldier is necessary, he loses everything and dies.

Part 5

Suggestions for
further reading

The text

The best edition currently available is the New Arden text edited by
Philip Brockbank, Methuen, London, 1976. It has detailed notes on
text and glossary, and a useful explanatory commentary. Its introduction
not only examines the play but mentions most of the books and articles
which have something useful to say about it. A less well annotated
edition is available in the New Penguin series, edited by G.R. Hibbard,
Penguin Books, Harmondsworth, 1967. The edition of the play in the
Riverside Shakespeare, Houghton Mifflin, Boston, 1974, a useful volume containing all the plays and poems, is also good value. References
to act, scene and line numbers in this study are taken from the New
Arden text.

Other works by Shakespeare

Coriolanus stands on its own at the end of the two long series, the
history plays beginning with *King John* and *1 Henry VI*, and the
tragedies beginning with *Julius Caesar* and *Hamlet*. The patterns of
political and human concerns set out with such astounding compactness
in *Coriolanus* are visible in all of these earlier plays. If any one play
can be linked to it more closely than any other, it must be *Antony and
Cleopatra*. The two were written at much the same time, and both use
material from Roman history which Shakespeare had ignored since
writing *Julius Caesar*. They make a striking pair in their parallels and
contrasts. *Antony* shows a great general destroyed through his love for
his mistress, while Coriolanus is destroyed in the end by his mother.
The two plays study contrasting sides of human personality, in contrasting worlds, contrasting language and contrasting political situa-
tions. Paul A. Cantor, *Shakespeare's Rome*, Cornell University Press,
Ithaca, 1976, p.13, even suggests that they should be studied as
companion pieces.

General reading

Background

BRADBROOK, M.C.: *Themes and Conventions of Elizabethan Tragedy*, Clarendon Press, Oxford, 1935. Outlines the main aspects of Elizabethan tragedy.

BULLOUGH, GEOFFREY (ed.): *Narrative and Dramatic Sources of Shakespeare*, 8 vols, Routledge, London, 1956–74, Vol. V. Prints all the sources for the play together with an essay on Shakespeare's use of them. The sources are also available in an appendix to the New Arden edition.

BURGESS, ANTONY: *Shakespeare*, Jonathan Cape, London, 1970. An entertaining and quite well-informed view of Shakespeare's life with some excellent illustrations.

GURR, ANDREW: *The Shakespearean Stage, 1574–1642*, Cambridge University Press, Cambridge, 1970. Describes the Elizabethan theatre, acting and audiences.

ONIONS, C.T.: *A Shakespeare Glossary*, Clarendon Press, Oxford, 1911. Lists all the entries in the Oxford English Dictionary relating to Shakespeare's use of words.

SCHOENBAUM, S.: *Shakespeare: a Documentary Life*, Clarendon Press, Oxford, 1975. The best biography.

Criticism

ALEXANDER, PETER (ed.): *Studies in Shakespeare*, British Academy, London, 1964.

BROCKMAN, B.A. (ed.): *Coriolanus*, Macmillan Casebook Series, Macmillan, London, 1977.

BROWER, REUBEN A.: *Hero and Saint: Shakespeare and the Graeco-Roman Heroic Tradition*, Clarendon Press, Oxford, 1971.

CANTOR, PAUL A.: *Shakespeare's Rome. Republic and Empire*, Cornell University Press, Ithaca, 1976.

DANSON, LAWRENCE: *Tragic Alphabet, Shakespeare's Drama of Language*, Yale University Press, New Haven, 1974.

VAN DYKE, JOYCE: 'Making a Scene: Language and Gesture in *Coriolanus*', *Shakespeare Survey* 30 (1977), pp.135–46.

ENRIGHT, D.J.: *The Apothecary's Shop*, Chatto, London, 1957.

GOLDMAN, MICHAEL: *Shakespeare and the Energies of Drama*, Princeton University Press, Princeton 1972.

GORDON, D.J.: 'Name and Fame: Shakespeare's *Coriolanus*' in *Papers, Mainly Shakespearian*, ed. G.I. Duthie, Aberdeen University Studies, Edinburgh, 1964.

GURR, ANDREW: '*Coriolanus* and the Body Politic', *Shakespeare Survey* 28 (1975), pp.63–9.

HUFFMAN, C.C.: *Coriolanus in Context*, Bucknell University Press, Lewisburg, 1972.

JORGENSEN, PAUL A.: *Shakespeare's Military World*, University of California Press, Berkeley, 1956.

KNIGHT, G. WILSON: *The Imperial Theme*, Chatto, London, 1931.

KNIGHTS, L.C.: *Some Shakespearian Themes*, Chatto, London, 1959.

PETTET, E.C.: '*Coriolanus* and the Midlands Insurrection of 1607', *Shakespeare Survey* 3 (1950), pp.34–42.

RABKIN, NORMAN: *Shakespeare and the Common Understanding*, Free Press, New York, 1967.

ROSSITER, A.P.: *Angel with Horns*, Chatto, London, 1961.

ZEEVELD, W.G.: '*Coriolanus* and Jacobean Politics', *Modern Language Review*, LVII (1962), pp.321–34.

The author of these notes

ANDREW GURR is Professor of English at Reading University. He has lectured at the Universities of Leeds, Nairobi (Kenya), Wellington (New Zealand) and Auckland (New Zealand). He has an MA from the University of Auckland, and a PH D from Cambridge University, where he also taught for several years. His publications include *The Shakespearean Stage* (1970), *'Hamlet' and the Distracted Globe* (1978), editions of plays by Beaumont and Fletcher, and critical articles on Shakespeare, as well as essays on the literature of Africa and New Zealand.